Edward Caswall, Catholic Church

Lyra Catholica

containing all the breviary and missal hymns, with others from various sources

Edward Caswall, Catholic Church

Lyra Catholica
containing all the breviary and missal hymns, with others from various sources

ISBN/EAN: 9783337361143

Printed in Europe, USA, Canada, Australia, Japan

Cover: Foto ©Lupo / pixelio.de

More available books at **www.hansebooks.com**

LYRA CATHOLICA:

CONTAINING

ALL THE BREVIARY AND MISSAL HYMNS,

WITH

OTHERS FROM VARIOUS SOURCES.

Translated by
EDWARD CASWALL, M.A.

DOMINE, DILEXI DECOREM DOMUS TUÆ.

BURNS & OATES

LONDON:
GRANVILLE MANSIONS,
28, ORCHARD STREET, W.

NEW YORK:
CATHOLIC PUBLICATION
SOCIETY CO.,
9, BARCLAY STREET.

MDCCCLXXXIV.

PREFACE.

"THE Breviary Office of the Church," remarks the reverend Author of the *Catholic Choralist*, "is, next to the august Sacrifice of the Altar, the most acceptable tribute of praise that man can offer to his Maker; and although, by reason of their various secular avocations, the laity are not bound, like the clergy, to its recital, yet that portion of it which includes the Hymns and Canticles might be frequently, if not daily, recited by them, with great spiritual benefit and fruit. Thus, besides the happiness of uniting with the Church in an important portion of her most acceptable service, the Faithful would become daily more and more enlightened on the sublime truths and mysteries of Religion, and furnished with the most pathetic and edifying subjects of instruction and meditation." He adds, that it was his wish to have inserted in his collection, together with the Vesper hymns which he gives, those also of Matins and Lauds, but that his engagements had not allowed him the necessary leisure for their translation, with the exception of a few only of the Matutinal hymns.

The want thus intimated, it has been the object of the present Translator to supply. How imperfectly he has succeeded in his task, none can feel more than himself; yet, circumstances having afforded him, during the past year, an unlooked-for amount of leisure, he thought he could not employ it more dutifully to the Church (feeling, at the same time, strongly attracted to the subject), than in an attempt to exhibit, for the first time in an English form, the entire series of those divine Hymns, which, in their Latin originals, have through ages been, and still continue to be, to countless saintly souls, the joy and consolation of their earthly pilgrimage.

The present contribution to the existing store of Catholic vernacular Hymns consists of three portions. The first, and by far the largest portion, comprehends all the Hymns in the Roman Breviary, including those in the Officia Sanctorum Angliæ. The second portion comprises the Hymns and Sequences of the Roman Missal; and the third consists of Hymns from various sources. Of these latter it may be observed, that the Hymns on the Nativity, Annunciation, and Visitation, of our Blessed Lady, as also those to St. Anne, St. Stephen, and St. John the Evangelist, are from the Monastic Breviary of Cluny; those on the Purification and the Assumption, the Hymn to Jesus, and that for Sunday Morning, from the Parisian Breviary; and those to St. Joseph, St. Peter, St. Paul, and St. Pius the Fifth, from the *Raccolta delle Indulgenze*. Every hymn, without exception, has been newly translated from the Latin; and there is reason to believe, that nearly half the hymns here given have never before appeared in the English tongue.

As respects the Hymns in general, it may be useful to remark, that the greater number of them appear to have been originally written, not with a view to private reading, but for the purpose of being sung to the beautiful ecclesiastical melodies by Monastic and other Religious Bodies at their Office in Choir. This circumstance will serve to explain a few scattered expressions which otherwise might seem unreal; as, for instance, where allusions occur to the practice of rising at midnight to sing praises to God;—and if, on the one hand, some few of the Hymns may so far appear less adapted to the use of persons living in the world, it is our gain surely, on the other hand, thus, by occasional glimpses, to be reminded of that more perfect life, which has never ceased to be a reality in the Catholic Church.

Another advantage, which we owe, doubtless, in a measure, to the same circumstance—an advantage not to be despised in a sentimental age —is the exceedingly plain and practical character of these Hymns. Written with a view to constant daily use, they aim at something more than merely exciting the feelings. They have a perpetual reference to action. Their character is eminently objective. Their tendency is, to take the individual out of himself; to set before him, in turn, all the varied and sublime Objects of Faith; and to blend him with the universal family of the Faithful. In this respect they utterly differ from the hymn-books of modern heretical bodies, which dwelling, as they do, almost entirely on the state and emotions of the individual, tend to inculcate the worst of all egotisms.

And here, although the Translator may seem to be pleading his own cause, yet he cannot refrain from observing, that truly poetical as are many of these Hymns, as indeed well befits the sacred outpourings of Christ's tender Spouse, still, as a whole, the devotional is their primary and least disappointing aspect. Whoever attempts to read them as mere poetry, will obtain from them little of that delight which they are capable of inspiring. And as this is true of the original Latin, so it is truer still of the Hymns as they appear in the present translation; in which, it is to be feared, the unadorned simplicity of the prototype has too often degenerated into plainness; while its beauties have been faintly reflected, and their clear edge blunted in passing through a too earthly medium.

Something still remains to be said respecting the Table prefixed to the present Collection. It may be observed, then, for the sake of those who are unacquainted with the subject, that several very important Feasts, as, for instance, those of the Blessed Virgin, of nearly all the Apostles, and of the English Saints, have no special Hymns of their own in the Roman Breviary, but draw their Hymns from the Common of Saints, whereas certain other Feasts of inferior rank have special Hymns attached to them. Hence it was found, that a mere statement of contents, however complete, would convey to the uninitiated eye a very inadequate and even erroneous view of the Catholic Festivals; and a

Calendar was accordingly chosen instead, both as serving to correct any such apparent disproportion in the Hymns, and also with the view of rendering them more readily serviceable for daily use, in the event of any person desiring so to employ them. By its aid, the very youngest readers will be able to follow, with sufficient exactness, the course of the ecclesiastical year; and happy indeed will the Translator be, if this little book may thus be permitted to have some share in fostering, among the youth of our Catholic Seminaries, that ecclesiastical spirit, which finds its true home nowhere but in the Catholic heart, and which, if it be not necessary to the soul, is assuredly a most lovely grace, and a powerful auxiliary of the Faith.

It will be observed, that on certain special Feasts, after a reference to the proper hymns in the Breviary, reference is also made, in the Table, to the Sequence for the day, where there happens to be one, as also to the Hymns from various sources. The object of this is, to give, at a single glance, all the Hymns in the Collection that belong to any particular Day, and, at the same time, to render the Calendar a complete table of reference to the entire contents of the volume.

As regards the terms used in this translation, it may be as well to notice, that the word *cultus*, in the few places where it occurs, has been translated *worship*, no other English term presenting itself as, on the whole, so highly authorized, or as so well expressing the character of that homage, supernatural though not divine, which the Christian soul takes delight in paying to the Angels and Saints, and to their blessed Queen.

In conclusion, the Translator desires to express here his warm thanks to those kind friends, both of the clergy and laity, who have assisted him in his work; as also his acknowledgments for the help which he has received from existing versions.

GENERAL CONTENTS.

	PAGE
TABLE AND CALENDAR	xv

Hymns from the Breviary.
Part I. HYMNS FOR THE WEEK . . 3
        Antiphons of the Blessed Virgin 38
Part II. HYMNS FROM THE PROPER OF THE SEASON . . . 48
Part III. HYMNS FROM THE PROPER OF SAINTS 127
Part IV. HYMNS FROM THE COMMON OF SAINTS 197

Hymns from the Missal. . . . 231

Hymns from various Sources.
At Benediction of the Blessed Sacrament 247
From the Office of the Immaculate Conception 255
Other Hymns 263

Super flumina Babylonis, illic sedimus et flevimus, cum
    recordaremur Sion.
Quomodo cantabimus canticum Domini in terra aliena ?
Si oblitus fuero tui, Jerusalem, oblivioni detur dextera
    mea.
Adhæreat lingua mea faucibus meis, si non meminero
    tui :
Si non proposuero Jerusalem in principio lætitiæ meæ.

Ps. 136.

A TABLE

SHOWING THE PROPER HYMNS FOR EVERY DAY THROUGH THE YEAR.

Arranged according to the English Calendar.

HYMNS FOR THE WEEK WHEN NOT OTHERWISE APPOINTED.

		PAGE
SUNDAY	Matins	3-5
	Lauds	6-8
	Vespers	13
	Hymns for Sunday Morning	293
MONDAY	Matins	14
	Lauds	15
	Vespers	17
TUESDAY	Matins	18
	Lauds	19
	Vespers	21
WEDNESDAY	Matins	22
	Lauds	23
	Vespers	24
THURSDAY	Matins	26
	Lauds	27
	Vespers	28

		PAGE
FRIDAY ..	Matins	29
	Lauds	31
	Vespers	32
SATURDAY ..	Matins	33
	Lauds	35
	Vespers	36
ON SUNDAYS AND WEEK-DAYS.		
	Prime	9
	Terce	10
	Sext	11
	None	12
	Compline	37

Antiphons of the Blessed Virgin.

From the first Sunday in Advent to the Feast of the
 Purification 38
From the Purification of the Blessed Virgin to Palm
 Sunday 39
From Easter Sunday to Whitsunday . . . 39
From Trinity Sunday to the last Sunday after Pen-
 tecost 40

HYMNS ON THE MOVEABLE FEASTS.

N.B.—*The Hymns at Second Vespers are the same as at First Vespers.*

	Vesp.	Mat.	Lauds.
Sundays and Week-days in Advent . *Page*	43	45	46
Friday after Septuagesima Sunday.			
Prayer of our Lord Jesus Christ on Mount Olivet	60	60	61
Friday after Sexagesima Sunday.			
The Passion of our Lord Jesus Christ .	63	65	66
Friday after Quinquagesima Sunday.			
The most holy Crown of Thorns of our Lord Jesus Christ . . .	68	68	69
Ash Wednesday, no special Hymns.			
First Sunday in Lent, and daily till Passion Sunday	70	72	74
Friday after the first Sunday in Lent.			
The Spear and Nails of our Lord Jesus Christ	75	76	77
Friday after the second Sunday in Lent.			
The most holy Winding Sheet of our Lord Jesus Christ . .	78	80	82

A TABLE OF HYMNS

	Vesp.	Mat.	Lauds.
Friday after the third Sunday in Lent. The most holy Five Wounds of our Lord Jesus Christ. Hymns as on Passion Sunday	89	91	93
Friday after the fourth Sunday in Lent. The most precious Blood of our Lord Jesus Christ	83	85	87
Passion Sunday and through the Week	89	91	93
Friday after Passion Sunday. The Seven Dolours of the Blessed Virgin Mary	138	140	141
Palm Sunday, and the Monday, Tuesday, and Wednesday following, as on Passion Sunday	89	91	93
Hymn sung on Palm Sunday, during the Procession before Mass, 231.			
Maunday Thursday, Hymn sung during the Procession after Mass, as at Vespers on the Feast of Corpus Christi, III.			
Good Friday, Hymn sung during the Adoration of the Cross, 233.			
Hymn of St. Francis Xavier, 295.			
Holy Saturday. For this day, as for the two preceding, there are no hymns in the Office of the Day.			

ON THE MOVEABLE FEASTS.

	Vesp.	Mat.	Lauds
Easter Sunday, and through the Week. No hymns in the Office of the Day.			
Sequence at Mass, 233.			
Hymn at Benediction of the Blessed Sacrament, 251.			
Low Sunday, and through Easter to Ascension-day	94	96	98
Ascension-day, and daily till Whitsunday .	100	101	100
Hymn to Jesus, 290.			
Whitsunday, and daily to Trinity Sunday .	103	104	106
Sequence at Mass, 234.			
Hymn to the Holy Ghost, 291.			
Trinity Sunday	108	109	110
Corpus Christi, and through the Octave .	111	113	114
Sequence at Mass, 236.			
Rhyme of St. Thomas Aquinas, 247.			
Prose, 249.			
Friday after the Octave of Corpus Christi.			
Feast of the most sacred Heart of Jesus	116	118	119
Another Office of the same Feast .	121	121	123
For hymns on the Sundays after Pentecost, *see* Hymns for the Week, p. xv.			

HYMNS BELONGING TO THE COMMON OF SAINTS.

		Vesp.	Mat.	Lauds.
On Feasts of the Blessed Virgin Mary	Page	197	199	200
Common of Apostles		202	204	202
In Easter		205	205	207
Of One Martyr		208	208	209
In Easter	210			
Of Many Martyrs		211	213	214
In Easter	215			
Of a Confessor and Bishop		216	216	217
Of a Confessor not a Bishop		216	216	219
Of Virgins		221	222	221
Of Holy Women		223	224	223
Of the Dedication of a Church		225	225	227

HYMNS FOR EACH MONTH.

N.B. Feasts of Obligation are marked in Roman letters—Feasts of Devotion in Italics.

ABBREVIATIONS.—Ap. Apostle—Bish. Bishop—Comm. Common—Conf. Confessor—Mart. Martyr—Virg. Virgin. An asterisk (*) implies that a change is to be made in the first stanza of *Iste Confessor*.

JANUARY.

1 CIRCUMCISION OF OUR LORD. Hymns as on Christmas-Day. Vesp. 48. Mat. 48. Lauds 49.
2 Octave-Day of St. Stephen. Comm. of one Mart. (See preceding page.)
3 Octave-Day of St. John the Evangelist. Comm. of Ap. (See preceding page.)
4 Octave-Day of Holy Innocents, as on the Day. Mat. 51. Lauds 52. Vesp. 52.
5 Octave-Day of St. Thomas of Canterbury, and Vigil of the Epiphany, as on Christmas-Day. Mat. 48. Lauds 49.
6 EPIPHANY OF OUR LORD, and during the Octave. Vesp. 53. Mat. 53. Lauds 54.
Second Sunday after Epiphany—
Feast of the most holy Name of Jesus. Vesp. 56. Mat. 57. Lauds 58.
13 Octave-Day of the Epiphany, as on the Day.
14 St. Hilary. Comm. of Conf. and Bish.*
15 St. Paul the first Hermit. Comm. of Conf. not Bish.*
16 St. Marcellus, Pope. Comm. of one Mart.
17 St. Anthony, Abbot. Comm. of Conf. not Bish.
18 St. Peter's Chair at Rome. Vesp. 127. Mat. 127. Lauds 128. Responsory of St. Peter, 277.

19 St. Wolstan. Comm. of Conf. and Bish.
20 SS. Fabian and Sebastian. Comm. of many Mart.
21 St. Agnes. Comm. of Virg. and Mart.
22 SS. Vincent and Anastasius. Comm. of many Mart.
23 Desponsation of B.V. Mary, as on her Feasts. (See page xx.)
24 St. Timothy, Bish. Comm. of one Mart.
25 Conversion of St. Paul. Vesp. 129. Mat. 129. Lauds from the Comm. of Ap. Responsory of St. Paul, 280.
26 St. Polycarp, Bish. Comm. of one Mart.
27 St. John Chrysostom. Comm. of Conf. and Bish.*
28 St. Raymund of Pennafort. Comm. of Conf. not Bish.*
29 St. Francis of Sales. Comm. of Conf. and Bish.*
30 St. Martina. Vesp. 130. Mat. 131. Lauds 132.
31 St. Peter Nolasco. Comm. of Conf. not Bish.*

FEBRUARY.

1 St. Ignatius, Bish. Comm. of one Mart.
2 *Purification of B.V. Mary*, or Candlemas-Day, as on her Feasts. Hymn on the Purification, 271.
3 St. Blase, Bish. Comm. of one Mart.
4 St. Andrew Corsini. Comm. of Conf. and Bish.*
5 St. Agatha. Comm. of Virg. and Mart.
6 St. Dorothy. Comm. of Virg. and Mart.
7 St. Romuald, Abbot. Comm. of Conf. not Bish.*
8 St. John of Matha. Comm. of Conf. not Bish.*
9 St. Apollonia. Comm. of Virg. and Mart.
10 St. Scholastica. Comm. of Virg. not Mart.
14 St. Valentine. Priest. Comm. of one Mart.
15 SS. Faustinus and Jovita. Comm. of many Mart.
18 St. Simeon, Bish. Comm. of one Mart.
22 St. Peter's Chair at Antioch, as at Rome. Vesp. 127. Mat. 127. Lauds 128.
23 St. Peter Damian. Comm. of Conf. and Bish.*
24 or 25 *St. Matthias.* Comm. of Ap.

MARCH.

1. St. David, Patron of Wales. Comm. of Conf. and Bish.
2. St. Chad. Comm. of Conf. and Bish.
4. St. Casimir. Comm. of Conf. not Bish.
7. St. Thomas of Aquin. Comm. of Conf. not Bish.
8. St. Felix. Ap. of the East Angles. Comm. of Conf. and Bish.
9. St. Frances, Widow. Comm. of Holy Women.
10. The Forty Martyrs. Comm. of many Mart.
11. St. John of God. Comm. of Conf. not Bish.
12. St. Gregory the Great, Pope, Ap. of England. Comm. of Conf. and Bish.
17. St. Patrick, Ap. of Ireland. Comm. of Conf. and Bish.
18. St. Gabriel the Archangel. Vesp. 133. Mat. 133. Lauds, first two and last two stanzas of All Saints, 191.
19. *St. Joseph, Spouse of B.V. Mary.* Vesp. 134. Mat. 136. Lauds 137. Responsory of St Joseph, 275.
20. St. Cuthbert. Comm. of Conf. and Bish.
21. St. Benedict, Abbot. Comm. of Conf. not Bish.
25. *Annunciation of B.V. Mary*, or Lady-Day, as on her Feasts. Hymns on the Annunciation, 267 and 268.

APRIL.

2. St. Francis of Paula. Comm. of Conf. not Bish.
3. St. Richard. Comm. of Conf. and Bish.
4. St. Isidore. Comm. of Conf. and Bish.
5. St. Vincent Ferrer. Comm. of Conf. not Bish.
11. St. Leo, Pope. Comm. of Conf. and Bish.
13. St. Hermenegild. Vesp. 142. Mat. 143. Lauds 142.
14. SS. Tiburtius, Valerian, and Maximus. Comm. of many Mart.
17. St. Anicetus, Pope. Comm. of one Mart.
21. St. Anselm. Comm. of Conf. and Bish.
22. SS. Soter and Caius. Comm. of many Mart.
23. *St. George, Protector of England.* Comm. of one Mart.
24. St. Fidelis of Sigmaringa. Comm. of one Mart.

25 St. Mark. Comm. of Ap.
26 SS. Cletus and Marcellinus. Comm. of many Mart.
27, 28 Within the Octave of St. George. as on Day.
29 St. Peter. Comm. of one Mart.
30 Octave-Day of St. George, as on Day.

MAY.

1 *SS. Philip and James.* Comm. of Ap.
2 St. Athanasius. Comm. of Conf. and Bish.
3 *Finding of the Holy Cross.* Hymns as on Passion Sunday. Vesp. 89. Mat. 91. Lauds 93.
4 St. Monica, Widow. Comm. of Holy Women.
5 St. Catherine of Sienna. Comm. of Virg. not Mart.
6 St. John before the Latin Gate. Comm. of Ap.
7 St. Stanislaus, Bish. Comm. of one Mart.
8 Apparition of St. Michael the Archangel. Vesp. 145. Mat. 145. Lauds, Christe sanctorum, 133.
9 St. Gregory Nazianzen. Comm. of Conf. and Bish.
10 St. Antoninus. Comm. of Conf. and Bish.*
11 St. Pius the Fifth, Pope. Comm. of Conf. and Bish.* Responsory of St. Pius the Fifth, 283.
12 SS. Nereus, Achilleus, and Domitella. Comm. of many Mart.
14 St. Boniface. Comm. of one Mart.
16 St. John Nepomucen. Comm. of one Mart.
17 St. Paschal Baylon. Comm. of Conf. not Bish.
18 St. Venantius. Vesp. 146. Mat. 148. Lauds 149.
19 St. Dunstan. Comm. of Conf. and Bish.
20 St. Bernardin. Comm. of Conf. not Bish.
21 St. Peter Celestin, Pope. Comm. of Conf. and Bish.
22 St. Ubaldus. Comm. of Conf. and Bish.
24 The B.V. Mary the help of Christians. Vesp. 150. Mat. 150. Lauds 152.
25 St. Aldhelm. Comm. of Conf. and Bish.
26 St. Augustine, Ap. of England. Comm. of Conf. and Bish.
27 St. Philip Neri. Comm. of Conf. not Bish.
28 St. Gregory the Seventh, Pope. Comm. of Conf. and Bish.

29 Within the Octave of St. Augustine, as on Day.
30 St. Felix, Pope. Comm. of one Mart.
31 St. Petronilla. Comm. of Virg. not Mart.

JUNE.

2 Octave-Day of St. Augustine, Ap. of England, as on Day.
3 ⁖St. Mary Magdalen of Pazzi. Comm. of Virg. not Mart.
4 St. Francis Caracciolo. Comm. of Conf. not Bish.
6 St. Norbert. Comm. of Conf. and Bish.
8 St. William. Comm. of Conf. and Bish.
9 SS. Primus and Felicianus. Comm. of many Mart.
10 St. Margaret, Queen of Scotland. Comm. of Holy Women.
11 St. Barnabas. Comm. of Ap.
12 St. John à Facundo. Comm. of Conf. not Bish.
13 St. Anthony of Padua. Comm. of Conf. not Bish.
14 St. Basil. Comm. of Conf. and Bish.*
15 SS. Vitus, Modestus, and Crescentia. Comm. of many Mart.
18 SS. Marcus and Marcellianus. Comm. of many Mart.
19 St. Juliana Falconieri. Vesp. 154. Mat. 154. Lauds, Comm. of Virg. not Mart.
20 St. Silverius, Pope. Comm. of one Mart.
21 St. Aloysius Gonzaga. Comm. of Conf. not Bish.
22 St. Alban, First Martyr of England. Comm. of one Mart.
24 *Nativity of St. John the Baptist.* Vesp. 155. Mat. 156. Lauds 158
25 St. William, Abbot. Comm. of Conf. not Bish.
26 SS. John and Paul. Comm. of many Mart.
27 Within the Octave of St. John the Baptist, as on Day.
28 St. Leo, Pope. Comm. of Conf. and Bish.
29 SS. PETER AND PAUL. Vesp. 159. Mat. Comm. of Ap. 204. Lauds, Beate pastor, 128, and Egregie doctor, 129.
30 Commemoration of St. Paul. Vesp. 129. Mat. 129. Lauds, Comm. of Ap.

JULY.

1 Octave-Day of St. John the Baptist, as on Day.
2 Visitation of B.V. Mary, as on her Feasts.
  Hymn on the Visitation, 270.
3, 4, 5 Within the Octave of SS. Peter and Paul. Comm. of Ap.
6 Octave-Day of SS. Peter and Paul. Comm. of Ap.
7 Translat. of St. Thomas of Canterbury. Comm. of one Mart.
8 St. Elizabeth, Q. of Portugal. Vesp. 160. Mat. 160. Lauds 161
10 Seven Brothers. Comm. of many Mart.
11 St. Pius. Pope, Comm. of one Mart.
12 St. John Gualbert, Abbot. Comm. of Conf. not Bish.
13 St. Anacletus, Pope. Comm. of one Mart.
14 St. Bonaventura. Comm. of Conf. and Bish.
15 Translation of St. Swithin. Comm. of Conf. and Bish.*
16 The B.V. Mary of Mount Carmel, as on her Feasts.
17 Translation of St. Osmund. Comm. of Conf. and Bish.*
18 St. Camillus de Lellis. Comm. of Conf. not Bish.*
19 St Vincent of Paul. Comm. of Conf. not Bish.*
20 St Jerome Emilian. Comm. of Conf. not Bish.*
21 St. Henry, Emperor. Comm. of Conf. not Bish.*
22 St. Mary Magdalen. Vesp. 162. Mat. 164. Lauds 164.
23 St Apolinaris. Comm. of one Mart.
24 St. Alexius, Comm. of Conf. not Bish.
25 *St. James the Greater.* Comm. of Ap.
26 *St. Anne, Mother of B.V. Mary.* Comm. of Holy Women. Hymn to St. Anne, 263.
27 St. Pantaleon. Comm. of one Mart.
28 SS. Nazarius, Celsus, and Victor. Comm. of many Mart.
29 St. Martha. Comm. of Virg. not Mart.
30 SS. Abdon and Sennen. Comm. of many Mart.
31 St. Ignatius Loyola. Comm. of Conf. not Bish.

AUGUST.

1 St. Peter's Chains. Vesp. 166. Mat. 127. Lauds 128.
2 St. Alphonsus Liguori. Comm. of Conf. and Bish.
3 Finding of St. Stephen, the First Martyr. Comm. of one Mart.
4 St. Dominic. Comm. of Conf. not Bish.*
5 The B.V. Mary ad Nives, as on her Feasts.
6 Transfiguration of our Lord. Vesp. 167. Mat. 167. Lauds 168.
7 St. Cajetan. Comm. of Conf. not Bish.
8 SS. Cyriacus, Largus, &c. Comm. of many Mart.
10 *St. Laurence.* Comm. of one Mart.
12 St. Clare. Comm. of Virg. not Mart.
13 Within the Octave of St. Laurence, as on Day.
15 ASSUMPTION OF B.V. MARY, as on her Feasts. Hymn on the Assumption, 273.
Sunday within the Octave of the Assumption—
St. Joachim, Father of B.V. Mary. Comm. of Conf. not Bish.*
16 St. Hyacinth. Comm. of Conf. not Bish.*
17 Octave-Day of St. Laurence. Comm. of one Mart.
20 St. Bernard, Abbot. Comm. of Conf. not Bish.
21 St. Jane Frances de Chantal, Widow. Comm. of Holy Women.
22 Octave-Day of the Assumption, as on Day.
23 St. Philip Benizi. Comm. of Conf. not Bish.
24 *St. Bartholomew.* Comm. of Ap.
25 St. Louis, King of France. Comm. of Conf. not Bish.
26 St. Zephyrinus, Pope. Comm. of one Mart.
27 St. Joseph Calasanctius. Comm. of Conf. not Bish.*
28 St. Augustine. Comm. of Conf. and Bish.
29 Beheading of St. John the Baptist. Comm. of one Mart.
30 St. Rose of Lima. Comm. of Virg. not Mart.
31 St. Aidan. Comm. of Conf. and Bish.

SEPTEMBER.

1. St. Raymund Nonnatus. Comm. of Conf. not Bish.*
2. St. Stephen, King of Hungary. Comm. of Conf. not Bish.+
5. St. Laurence Justinian. Comm. of. Conf. and Bish.*
8. *Nativity of B.V. Mary*, as on her Feasts. Hymn on the Nativity of B.V. Mary, 265.
   Sunday within the Octave.
   The most holy Name of B.V. Mary, as on her Feasts.
9. Within the Octave of the Nativity of B.V.M. as on Day.
10. St. Nicholas of Tolentinum. Comm. of Conf. not Bish.
14. Exaltation of the Holy Cross, as on Passion-Sunday. Vesp. 89. Mat. 91. Lauds 93.
15. Octave-Day of the Nativity of B.V.M. as on Day.
    Third Sunday in September—
        The Seven Dolours of B.V. Mary. Vesp. 169. Mat. 171. Lauds 173.
16. SS. Cornelius and Cyprian. Comm. of many Mart.
17. Stigmas of St. Francis. Comm. of Conf. not Bish.
18. St. Joseph of Cupertino. Comm. of Conf. not Bish.
19. St. Januarius and Companions. Comm. of many Mart.
20. St. Eustachius and Companions. Comm. of many Mart.
21. *St. Matthew.* Comm. of Ap.
22. St. Thomas of Villanova. Comm. of Conf. and Bish.*
23. St. Linus, Pope. Comm. of one Mart.
24. The B.V. Mary of Mercy, as on her Feasts.
26. SS. Cyprian and Justina. Comm. of many Mart.
27. SS. Cosmas and Damian. Comm. of many Mart.
28. St. Winceslaus, Duke. Comm. of one Mart.
29. *Dedication of St. Michael.* Vesp. 145. Mat. 145. Lauds, Christe sanctorum, 133.
30. St. Jerome. Comm. of Conf. not Bish.

CALENDAR. xxix

OCTOBER.

First Sunday in October—
　　The Most Holy Rosary of B.V. Mary, as on her Feasts.
1　St. Remigius. Comm. of Conf. and Bish.*
2　The Holy Guardian Angels. Vesp. 174. Mat. 174. Lauds 175.
3　St. Thomas of Hereford. Comm. of Conf. and Bish.
4　St. Francis of Assisium. Comm. of Conf. not Bish.
5　St. Placidus and Companions. Comm. of many Mart.
6　St. Bruno. Comm. of Conf. not Bish.
7　St. Mark, Pope. Comm. of Conf. and Bish.
Second Sunday in October—
　　Maternity of B.V. Mary. Mat. 177. Lauds 178. Vesp. as on her Feasts.
8　St. Bridget. Comm. of Holy Women.
9　SS. Dionysius, Rusticus, and Eleutherius. Comm. of many Mart.
10　St. Paulinus, Archbishop of York. Comm. of Conf. and Bish.
11　St. Francis Borgia. Comm. of Conf. not Bish.*
12　St. Wilfrid. Comm. of Conf. and Bish.
13　Translation of St. Edward, King and Confessor. Comm. of Conf. not Bish.*
14　St. Callistus, Pope. Comm. of one Mart.
Third Sunday in October—
　　Purity of B.V. Mary. Vesp. 179. Mat. 181. Lauds as on her Feasts.
15　St. Teresa. Vesp. 182. Mat. 183. Lauds 182.
16　Within the Octave of St. Edward, as on Day.
17　St. Hedwiges. Comm. of Holy Women.
18　St. Luke. Comm. of Ap.
19　St. Peter of Alcantara. Comm. of Conf. not Bish. *
20　Octave-Day of St. Edward, as on Day.
21　St. Ursula and Companions. Comm. of Virg. and Mart.
Fourth Sunday in October—
　　Patronage of B.V. Mary, as on her Feasts.
22　St. John Cantius. Vesp. 184. Mat. 186. Lauds 187.
23　Feasts of our Most Holy Redeemer. Vesp. Creator alme 43. Mat. Rerum Creator 22. Lauds, Salutis humanæ 100.

24 St. Raphael the Archangel. Vesp. 188. Mat. 188. Lauds 190.
25 St. John of Beverly. Comm. of Conf. and Bish.
26 St. Evaristus, Pope. Comm. of one Mart.
28 *SS. Simon and Jude.* Comm. of Ap.
29 Venerable Bede. Comm. of Conf. not Bish.*

NOVEMBER.

1 ALL SAINTS. Vesp. 191. Mat. 191. Lauds 193.
2 All Souls. No hymn in the Office of the Day. Sequence in Mass for the Dead, 241.
3 St. Winefrid. Comm. of Virg. and Mart.
4 St. Charles Borromeo. Comm. of Conf. and Bish.
5, 6, 7 Within the Octave of all Saints, as on Day.
8 Octave-Day of All Saints, as on Day.
9 Dedication of the Basilica of our Saviour. Comm. of the Dedication of a Church.
10 St. Andrew Avellino. Comm. of Conf. not Bish.
11 St. Martin. Comm. of Conf. and Bish.
12 St. Martin, Pope. Comm. of one Mart.
13 St. Didacus. Comm. of Conf. not Bish.
14 Translation of St. Erconwald. Comm. of Conf. and Bish.*
15 St. Gertrude. Comm. of Virg. not Mart.
16 St. Edmund. Comm. of Conf. and Bish.
17 St. Hugh. Comm. of Conf. and Bish.
18 Dedication of the Basilica of SS. Peter and Paul. Comm. of the Dedication of a Church.
19 St. Elizabeth. Comm. of Holy Women.
20 St. Edmund, King. Comm. of one Mart.
21 Presentation of B.V. Mary, as on her Feasts.
22 St. Cecilia. Comm. of Virg. and Mart.
23 St. Clement, Pope. Comm. of one Mart.
24 St. John of the Cross. Comm. of Conf. not Bish.*
25 St. Catherine. Comm. of Virg. and Mart.
26 St. Felix of Valois. Comm. of Conf. not Bish.*
27 St. Gregory Thaumaturgus. Comm. of Conf. and Bish.
29 St. Saturninus. Comm. of one Mart.
30 *St. Andrew.* Comm. of Ap.

DECEMBER.

2 St. Bibiana. Comm. of Virg. and Mart.
3 St. Francis Xavier. Comm. of Conf. not Bish.
4 St. Peter Chrysologus. Comm. of Conf. and Bish.*
5 St. Birinus. Comm. of Conf. and Bish.
6 St. Nicholas of Myra. Comm. of Conf. and Bish.
7 St. Ambrose. Comm. of Conf. and Bish.*
8 *Conception of B.V. Mary*, as on her Feasts.
   Hymns from the Office of the Immaculate Conception, 255.
9, 10 Within the Octave of the Conception, as on Day.
11 St. Damasus, Pope. Comm. of Conf. and Bish.
12 Within the Octave of the Conception, as on Day.
13 St. Lucy. Comm. of Virg. and Mart.
15 Octave-Day of the Conception, as on Day.
16 St. Eusebius, Bish. Comm. of one Mart.
18 Expectation of B.V. Mary, as on First Sunday in Advent. Vesp. 43. Mat. 45. Lauds 46.
21 *St. Thomas.* Comm. of Ap.
25 NATIVITY OF OUR LORD. Vesp. 48. Mat. 48. Lauds 49.
    Hymn on Christmas-Day, 250.
        Memento rerum Conditor, 201.
26 *St. Stephen*, the First Martyr. Comm. of one Mart.
    Hymn to St. Stephen, 285.
27 *St. John the Evangelist.* Comm. of Ap.
    Hymns to St. John, 287 and 289.
28 *Holy Innocents.* Mat. 51. Lauds 52. Vesp. 52.
29 *St. Thomas of Canterbury.* Comm. of one Mart.
30 Within the Octave of the Nativity, as on Day.
31 St. Sylvester. Comm. of Conf. and Bish.

Let the word of Christ dwell in you abundantly, in all wisdom: teaching and admonishing one another in psalms, hymns, and spiritual canticles, singing in grace in your hearts to God.

Epistle of St. Paul to the Colossians.

HYMNS FROM THE BREVIARY.

Part I.

HYMNS FOR THE WEEK.

HYMNS FROM THE BREVIARY.

Part I.

HYMNS FOR THE WEEK.

Sunday.

MATINS.

Primo die quo Trinitas.

This day the glorious Trinity
　Creation's work began;
This day the world's Creator rose,
　O'ercoming death for man.

HYMNS FOR THE WEEK.

Casting betimes dull sloth away,
   We too will rise by night;
And with the Prophet seek the Lord,
   Before the dawning light.

So may He stretch His hand to save
   And hear us in His love;
And renovate us by His grace,
   For our true home above.

So, while on this His holy Day,
   At this most sacred hour,
Our psalms amid the stillness rise,
   May He His blessings shower.

Father of lights! keep us this day
   From sinful passions free;
Grant us, in every word, and deed,
   And thought, to honour Thee.

Assist us, Purity divine,
   Within our hearts to quell
Those evil fires which, cherish'd here,
   Augment the flames of hell.

Saviour, of Thy sweet clemency,
   Wash Thou our sins away;
Grant us Thy peace—grant us with Thee
   Thine own eternal day.

Father of mercies! hear our cry;
   Hear us, coequal Son!
Who reignest, with the Holy Ghost,
   While endless ages run.

From the Octave of Pentecost to the Sunday nearest the first of October.

Nocte surgentes vigilemus omnes.

Let us arise and watch ere dawn of light,
And to the Lord our hearts and voices raise;
And meditate in psalms, and all unite
   In holy hymns of praise.

So, blending here our strains to God on high,
Hereafter, in the courts of Heaven's great King,
May we be meet His praise eternally
   Among His Saints to sing.

Father supreme! this grace on us confer,
And Thou, O Son, by an eternal birth!
With Thee, coequal Spirit Comforter!
   Whose glory fills the earth.

LAUDS.

Æterne rerum conditor.

DREAD Framer of the earth and sky!
   Who dost the circling seasons give!
And all the cheerful change supply
   Of alternating morn and eve!

Light of our darksome journey here,
   With days dividing night from night!—
Loud crows the dawn's shrill harbinger,
   And wakens up the sunbeams bright.

Forthwith at this, the darkness chill
   Retreats before the star of morn;
And from their busy schemes of ill,
   The vagrant crews of night return.

Fresh hope, at this, the sailor cheers ;
    The waves their stormy strife allay ;
The Church's Rock at this, in tears,
    Hastens to wash his guilt away.

Arise ye, then, with one accord !
    Nor longer wrapt in slumber lie ;
The cock rebukes all who their Lord
    By sloth neglect, by sin deny.

At his clear cry joy springs afresh ;
    Health courses through the sick man's veins ;
The dagger glides into its sheath ;
    The fallen soul her faith regains.

Jesu ! look on us when we fall ;—
    One momentary glance of Thine
Can from her guilt the soul recall
    To tears of penitence divine.

Awake us from false sleep profound,
    And through our senses pour Thy light;
Be Thy blest name the first we sound
    At early dawn, the last at night.

To God the Father glory be,
  And to His sole-begotten Son;
Glory, O Holy Ghost! to Thee,
  While everlasting ages run.

From the Octave of Pentecost to the Sunday nearest the first of October.

Ecce jam noctis tenuatur umbra.

Lo, fainter now lie spread the shades of night,
And upward shoot the trembling gleams of morn:
Suppliant we bend before the Lord of Light,
  And pray at early dawn,—

That His sweet charity may all our sin
Forgive, and make our miseries to cease;
May grant us health of soul, grant us delights
  Of everlasting peace.

Father supreme! this grace on us confer;
And Thou, O Son, by an eternal birth!
With Thee, coequal Spirit Comforter!
  Whose glory fills the earth.

HYMN AT PRIME.

On Sundays and Week-days throughout the Year.

Jam lucis orto sidere.

Now doth the sun ascend the sky,
   And wake creation with its ray;
Keep us from sin, O Lord most high!
   Through all the actions of the day.

Curb Thou for us th' unruly tongue;
   Teach us the way of peace to prize;
And close our eyes against the throng
   Of earth's absorbing vanities.

Oh, may our hearts be pure within!
   No cherish'd madness vex the soul!
May abstinence the flesh restrain,
   And its rebellious pride control.

So when the evening stars appear,
   And in their train the darkness bring;
May we, O Lord, with conscience clear,
   Our praise to Thy pure glory sing.

To God the Father glory be,
  And to His sole-begotten Son;
Glory, O Holy Ghost! to Thee,
  While everlasting ages run.

HYMN AT TERCE.
On Sundays and Week-days throughout the Year.
Nunc Sancte nobis Spiritus.

Come, Holy Ghost, and through each heart
  In Thy full flood of glory pour;
Who, with the Son and Father art
  One Godhead blest for evermore.

So shall voice, mind, and strength conspire
  Salvation's anthem to resound;
So shall our hearts be set on fire,
  And kindle every heart around.

Father of mercies! hear our cry;
  Hear us, O sole-begotten Son!
Who, with the Holy Ghost most high,
  Reignest while endless ages run.

HYMN AT SEXT.

On Sundays and Week-days throughout the Year.

Rector potens, verax Deus.

Lord of eternal truth and might!
  Ruler of Nature's changing scheme!
Who dost bring forth the morning light,
  And temper noon's effulgent beam:

Quench Thou in us the flames of strife,
  And bid the heat of passion cease;
From perils guard our feeble life,
  And keep our souls in perfect peace.

Father of mercies! hear our cry;
  Hear us, O sole-begotten Son!
Who, with the Holy Ghost most high,
  Reignest while endless ages run.

HYMN AT NONE.

On Sundays and Week-days throughout the Year.

Rerum Deus tenax vigor.

O Thou true life of all that live!
 Who dost, unmoved, all motion sway
Who dost the morn and evening give,
 And through its changes guide the day:

Thy light upon our evening pour,—
 So may our souls no sunset see;
But death to us an open door
 To an eternal morning be.

Father of mercies! hear our cry;
 Hear us, O sole-begotten Son!
Who, with the Holy Ghost most high,
 Reignest while endless ages run.

HYMN AT VESPERS.

On Sunday when no other Hymn is appointed.

Lucis Creator optime.

O BLEST Creator of the light!
  Who dost the dawn from darkness bring;
And framing Nature's depth and height,
  Didst with the light Thy work begin;

Who, gently blending eve with morn,
  And morn with eve, did'st call them day;—
Thick flows the flood of darkness down;
  Oh, hear us as we weep and pray!

Keep Thou our souls from schemes of crime:
  Nor guilt remorseful let them know;
Nor, thinking but on things of time,
  Into eternal darkness go.

Teach us to knock at Heaven's high door;
  Teach us the prize of life to win;
Teach us all evil to abhor,
  And purify ourselves within.

Father of mercies! hear our cry;
   Hear us, O sole-begotten Son!
Who, with the Holy Ghost most high,
   Reignest while endless ages run.

Monday.

MATINS.

Somno refectis artubus.

Our limbs with tranquil sleep refresh'd,
   Lightly from bed we spring;
Father supreme! to us be nigh,
   While in Thy praise we sing.

Thy love be first in every heart,
   Thy name on every tongue;
Whatever we this day may do,
   May it in Thee be done.

Soon will the morning star arise,
   And chase the dusk away;
The guilt that may have come with night,
   May it depart with day.

Cut off in us whatever root
   Of sin or shame there be;
So evermore from bosoms pure
   Be rendered praise to Thee.

Father of mercies! hear our cry;
   Hear us, coequal Son!
Who reignest, with the Holy Ghost,
   While endless ages run.

LAUDS.

Splendor paternæ gloriæ.

O Thou the Father's Image blest!
   Who callest forth the morning ray;
O Thou eternal Light of light!
   And inexhaustive Fount of day!

True Sun!—upon our souls arise,
   Shining in beauty evermore;
And through each sense the quick'ning beam
   Of Thy eternal Spirit pour.

Thee too, O Father, we entreat,
  Father of might and grace divine!
Father of glorious majesty!
  Thy pitying eye on us incline.

Confirm us in each good resolve;
  The Tempter's envious rage subdue;
Turn each misfortune to our good;
  Direct us right in all we do.

Rule Thou our inmost thoughts; let no
  Impurity our hearts defile;
Grant us a sober heart and mind;
  Grant us a spirit free from guile.

May Christ Himself be our true Food,
  And Faith our daily cup supply;
While from the Spirit's tranquil depth
  We drink unfailing draughts of joy.

Still ever, pure as morn's first ray,
  May modesty our steps attend;
Our faith be fervent as the noon;
  Upon our souls no night descend.

Fast breaks the dawn.—Each whole in Each,
  Come, Father blest! come, Son most High!
Shine in our souls, and be to them
  The dawn of Immortality.

To God the Father glory be,
  And to His sole-begotten Son;
Glory, O Holy Ghost! to Thee,
  While everlasting ages run.

VESPERS.

Immense cæli conditor.

LORD of immensity sublime!
  Who, lest the waters should confound
Thy world, didst them in earliest time
  Divide, and make the skies their bound;

Framing for some on earth below,
  For others in the heavens a place;
That, tempered thus, the sun's hot glow
  Might not Thy beauteous works efface.

c

Upon our fainting souls distil
  The grace of Thy celestial dew;
Let no fresh snare to sin beguile,
  No former sin revive anew.

Grant us the grace, for love of Thee,
  To scorn all vanities below;
Faith, to detect each falsity;
  And knowledge, Thee alone to know.

Father of mercies! hear our cry;
  Hear us, O sole-begotten Son!
Who, with the Holy Ghost most high,
  Reignest while endless ages run.

Tuesday.

MATINS.

Consors paterni luminis.

PURE Light of light! eternal Day,
  Who dost the Father's brightness share;
Our chant the midnight silence breaks;—
  Be nigh, and hearken to our prayer.

Scatter the darkness of our minds,
    And turn the hosts of hell to flight;
Let not our souls in sloth repose,
    And sleeping sink in endless night.

O Christ! for Thy dear mercy's sake,
    Spare us, who put our trust in Thee;
Nor let our early hymn ascend
    In vain to Thy pure Majesty.

Father of mercies! hear our cry;
    Hear us, O sole-begotten Son!
Who, with the Holy Ghost most high,
    Reignest while endless ages run.

LAUDS.

Ales diei nuntius.

Now, while the herald bird of day
    Announces morning bright;
Christ also, speaking in the soul,
    Wakes her to life and light.

'Take up your beds,' we hear Him say,
  'No more in slumber lie;
In justice, truth, and temperance,
  Keep watch;—your Lord is nigh.'

O Jesus! art Thou nigh indeed?—
  Then let us watch and weep;
This truth but once in earnest felt
  Forbids the heart to sleep.

Break, Lord, the spell that wraps us round
  In deadly bonds of night;
Unbind the chains of former guilt;
  Renew in us Thy light.

To God the Father glory be,
  And sole eternal Son;
And glory, Holy Ghost! to Thee,
  While endless ages run.

VESPERS.

Telluris alme conditor.

O BOUNTEOUS Framer of the globe!
  Who with Thy mighty hand
Didst gather up the rolling seas,
  And firmly base the land:

That so the freshly teeming earth
  Might herb and seedling bear
All in their early beauty gay
  With flowers and fruitage fair

On our parch'd souls pour Thou, O Lord,
  The freshness of Thy grace;
So penitence shall spring anew,
  And all the past efface.

Grant us to fear Thy holy law,
  To feel Thy goodness nigh:
Grant us through life Thy peace; in death
  Thine immortality.

Father of mercies! hear our cry;
　Hear us, coequal Son!
Who reignest, with the Holy Ghost,
　While endless ages run.

Wednesday.
MATINS.
Rerum Creator optime.

O BLEST Creator of the world!
　Look in compassion down;
Nor let the guilty sleep of sin
　Our souls in torpor drown.

Lord of all holiness! may we
　Have favour in Thy sight;
Who, to set forth Thy glory, rise
　Before the morning light.

Who, as the holy Psalmist bids,
　Our hands thus early raise;
And in the midnight sing with Paul
　And Silas hymns of praise.

Jesu! to Thee our deeds we show,
  To Thee our hearts lie bare;
Oh, hearken to the sighs we send,
  And in Thy pity spare.

Father of mercies! hear our cry;
  Hear us, coequal Son!
Who reignest, with the Holy Ghost,
  While endless ages run.

LAUDS.

Nox et tenebra et nubila.

YE mist and darkness, cloud and storm,
  Confused creations of the night;—
Light enters—morning streaks the sky—
  Christ comes,—'tis time ye took your flight.

Pierced by the sun's ethereal dart,
  Night's gloomy mass is cleft in twain;
And, in the smiling face of day,
  Nature resumes her tints again.

O Christ, we know no sun but Thee!
  Shine in our souls divinely bright!
We seek Thee in simplicity;
  Through all our senses shed Thy light.

A thousand objects all around
  In false, delusive colours shine;
To purge them clear, we ask, dear Lord,
  But one immortal beam of Thine.

To God the Father glory be,
  And to His sole-begotten Son;
Glory, O Holy Ghost! to Thee,
  While everlasting ages run.

VESPERS.

Cæli Deus sanctissime.

LORD of eternal purity!
  Who dost the world with light adorn,
And paint the fields of azure sky
  With lovely hues of eve and morn;

Who didst command the sun to light
   His fiery wheel's effulgent blaze;
Didst set the moon her circuit bright;
   The stars their ever-winding maze:

That, each within its order'd sphere,
   They might divide the night from day;
And of the seasons, through the year,
   The well remember'd signs display:

Scatter our night, eternal God,
   And kindle Thy pure beam within;
Free us from guilt's oppressive load,
   And break the deadly bonds of sin.

Father of mercies! hear our cry;
   Hear us, O sole-begotten Son!
Who, with the Holy Ghost most high,
   Reignest while endless ages run.

Thursday.

MATINS.

Nox atra rerum contegit.

The pall of night o'ershades the earth,
    And hides the tints of day;—
O Thou! to whom no night comes near,
    Dread Judge! to Thee we pray:

That all our guilt Thou wilt remove,
    And our lost peace restore;
And of Thy mercy grant us grace
    Thee to offend no more.

The guilty soul, which all too long
    In lethargy hath lain,
Yearns to cast off her load, and seek
    Her Saviour's face again.

Expel from her the darkness, Lord,
    Of her internal night;
Renew her bliss—renew in her
    Thy beatific light.

Father of mercies! hear our cry;
   Hear us, coequal Son!
Who reignest, with the Holy Ghost,
   While endless ages run.

LAUDS.

Lux ecce surgit aurea.

Now with the rising golden dawn,
   Let us, the children of the day,
Cast off the darkness which so long
   Has led our guilty souls astray.

Oh, may the morn so pure, so clear,
   Its own sweet calm in us instil;
A guileless mind, a heart sincere,
   Simplicity of word and will:

And ever, as the day glides by,
   May we the busy senses rein;
Keep guard upon the hand and eye,
   Nor let the body suffer stain.

For all day long, on Heaven's high tower,
   There stands a Sentinel, who spies
Our every action, hour by hour,
   From early dawn till daylight dies.

To God the Father glory be,
   And to His sole-begotten Son;
Glory, O Holy Ghost! to Thee,
   While everlasting ages run.

VESPERS.

Magnæ Deus potentiæ.

LORD of all power! at whose command,
   The waters, from their teeming womb,
Brought forth the countless tribes of fish,
   And birds of every note and plume:

Who didst, for natures link'd in birth,
   Far different homes of old prepare;
Sinking the fishes in the sea;
   Lifting the birds aloft in air:

Lo! born of Thy baptismal wave,
  We ask of Thee, O Lord divine!
'Keep us, whom Thou hast sanctified
  In Thy own Blood, for ever Thine.

Safe from all pride, as from despair;
  Not sunk too low, nor raised too high;
Lest, raised by pride, we headlong fall;
  Sunk in despair lie down and die.'

Father of mercies! hear our cry;
  Hear us, O sole-begotten Son!
Who, with the Holy Ghost most high,
  Reignest while endless ages run.

Friday.

MATINS.

Tu Trinitatis Unitas.

O THOU! Who dost all Nature sway,
  Dread Trinity in Unity!
Accept the trembling praise we pay
  To Thy eternal Majesty.

For one and all we now arise,
   While solemn midnight breathes around,
To seek from Thee, with tears and sighs,
   A healing balm of every wound.

Almighty Lord! whatever guilt
   Satan hath wrought in us this night,
Oh may it now before Thee melt
   As mist before the morning light.

Grant us a body pure within;
   A wakeful heart, a ready will;
Grant us, by no deep cherish'd sin,
   The fervour of the soul to chill.

Kindle our minds, Redeemer true,
   With Thy most pure celestial ray;
So may we walk in safety through
   All the temptations of the day.

Father of mercies! hear our cry;
   Hear us, O sole-begotten Son!
Who, with the Holy Ghost most high,
   Reignest while endless ages run.

LAUDS.

Æterna cæli gloria.

Eternal Glory of the heavens!
  Blest Hope of all on earth!
God, of eternal Godhead born!
  Man, by a virgin birth!

Jesu! be near us when we wake;
  And, at the break of day,
With Thy blest touch arouse the soul,
  Her meed of praise to pay.

The star that heralds in the morn
Is fading in the skies;
The darkness melts;—O Thou, true Light,
  Once more on us arise.

Steep all our senses in Thy beam;
  The world's false night expel;
Purge each defilement from the soul,
  And in our bosoms dwell.

Come, early Faith! fix in our hearts
  Thy root immovably;
Come, smiling Hope! and, greater still,
  Come, heaven-born Charity!

To God the Father glory be,
  And sole eternal Son;
And glory, Holy Ghost! to Thee,
  While endless ages run.

VESPERS.

Hominis supernє conditor.

Maker of men! who First and Sole,
  All things in wisdom ordering,
Didst from the teeming earth bring forth
  Wild beasts, and every creeping thing:

At whose command, instinct with life,
  Huge forms emerged from shapeless clay;
Ordain'd, through their appointed times,
  Man, Thy frail servant, to obey

Expel from us wild passions, Lord,
  With all the reptile brood of sin;
Nor suffer vice, familiar grown,
  To make itself a home within.

Hereafter grant thine endless joys;
  Here thy continual grace supply;
Unweave the guilty web of strife;
  Draw close the bonds of unity.

Father of mercies! hear our cry;
  Hear us, O sole-begotten Son!
Who, with the Holy Ghost most high,
  Reignest while endless ages run.

Saturday.

MATINS.

Summæ Parens clementiæ.

O THOU eternal Source of love!
  Ruler of Nature's scheme!
In Substance One, in Persons Three!
  Omniscient and Supreme!

For thy dear mercy's sake receive
　　The strains and tears we pour,
And purify our hearts to taste
　　Thy sweetness more and more.

Our flesh, our reins, our spirits, Lord,
　　In thy clear fire refine;
Break down the self-indulgent will;
　　Gird us with strength divine.

So may all we, who here are met
　　By night thy name to bless,
One day, in our eternal home,
　　Thy promises possess.

Father of mercies! hear our cry;
　　Hear us, coequal Son!
Who reignest with the Holy Ghost
　　While endless ages run.

LAUDS.

Aurora jam spargit polum.

The dawn is sprinkling in the East
   Its golden shower, as day flows in;
Fast mount the pointed shafts of light;—
   Farewell to darkness and to sin!

Away, ye midnight phantoms all!
   Away, despondence and despair!
Whatever guilt the night has brought,
   Now let it vanish into air.

So, Lord, when that last morning breaks
   Looking to which we sigh and pray,
O may it to thy minstrels prove
   The dawning of a better day.

To God the Father glory be,
   And to his sole-begotten Son;
Glory, O Holy Ghost! to Thee,
   While everlasting ages run.

VESPERS.

Jam sol recedit igneus.

Now doth the fiery sun decline:—
    Thou, Unity Eternal! shine;
Thou, Trinity! thy blessings pour,
    And make our hearts with love run o'er.

Thee in the hymns of morn we praise;
To Thee our voice at eve we raise;
O grant us, with thy Saints on high,
Thee through all time to glorify.

Praise to the Father, with the Son,
    And Holy Spirit, Three in One;
As ever was in ages past,
    And so shall be while ages last.

———

The Hymns at Matins, Lauds, and Vespers, during Lent and Easter, will be found among those belonging to the Proper of the Season.

———

HYMN AT COMPLINE.

On Sundays and Week-days throughout the Year.

Te lucis ante terminum.

Now with the fast-departing light,
   Maker of all! we ask of Thee,
Of thy great mercy, through the night
   Our guardian and defence to be.

Far off let idle visions fly;
   No phantom of the night molest:
Curb thou our raging enemy,
   That we in chaste repose may rest.

Father of mercies! hear our cry;
   Hear us, O sole-begotten Son!
Who, with the Holy Ghost most high,
   Reignest while endless ages run.

ANTIPHONS
OF THE BLESSED VIRGIN.

From the First Sunday in Advent to the Feast of the Purification.

Alma Redemptoris Mater.

Mother of Christ! hear thou thy people's cry,
Star of the deep, and Portal of the sky!
Mother of Him who thee from nothing made.
Sinking we strive, and call to thee for aid:
Oh, by that joy which Gabriel brought to thee,
Pure Virgin, first and last, look on our misery.

From the Purification of the Blessed Virgin to Palm Sunday.

Ave Regina cælorum.

Hail, O Queen of Heav'n, enthroned!
Hail, by angels Mistress own'd!
Root of Jesse! Gate of morn!
Whence the world's true Light was born:
Glorious Virgin, joy to thee,
Beautiful surpassingly!
Fairest thou, where all are fair!
Plead for us a pitying prayer.

From Easter-Sunday to Whit-Sunday.

Regina cœli lætare.

Joy to thee, O Queen of Heaven! Alleluia.
  He whom it was thine to bear; Alleluia.
As He promised, hath arisen; Alleluia.
  Plead for us a pitying prayer; Alleluia.

From Trinity Sunday to the last Sunday after Pentecost.

Salve, Regina, Mater misericordiæ.

MOTHER of mercy, hail, O gracious Queen!
Our life, our sweetness, and our hope, all hail!
    Children of Eve,
To thee we cry from our sad banishment;
    To thee we send our sighs,
Weeping and mourning in this vale of tears.
    Come, then, our Advocate;
Oh, turn on us those pitying eyes of thine:
    And our long exile past,
      Show us at last
Jesus, of thy pure womb the fruit divine.
    O Virgin Mary, mother blest!
    O sweetest, gentlest, holiest!

HYMNS FROM THE BREVIARY.

Part II.

HYMNS BELONGING TO THE PROPER OF THE SEASON.

HYMNS FROM THE BREVIARY.

Part II.

HYMNS BELONGING TO THE PROPER OF THE YEAR.

On Sundays and Week-days during Advent.

VESPERS.

Creator alme siderum.

Dear Maker of the starry skies!
   Light of believers evermore
Jesu, Redeemer of mankind!
   Be near us who thine aid implore.

When man was sunk in sin and death,
   Lost in the depth of Satan's snare,
Love brought Thee down to cure our ills,
   By taking of those ills a share.

Thou, for the sake of guilty men
   Permitting thy pure blood to flow,
Didst issue from thy Virgin shrine
   And to the Cross a Victim go.

So great the glory of thy might,
   If we but chance thy name to sound,
At once all Heaven and Hell unite
   In bending low with awe profound.

Great Judge of all! in that last day,
   When friends shall fail, and foes combine,
Be present then with us, we pray,
   To guard us with thy arm divine.

To God the Father, with the Son,
   And Holy Spirit, One and Three,
Be honour, glory, blessing, praise,
   All through the long eternity.

PROPER OF THE SEASON.

[Within the Octave of the Feast of the Conception.]

O Jesu! born of Virgin bright,
    Immortal glory be to Thee;
Praise to the Father infinite,
    And Holy Ghost eternally.

MATINS.

Verbum supernum prodiens.

O Thou, who thine own Father's breast
    Forsaking, Word Sublime!
Didst come to aid a world distress'd
    In thy appointed time:

Our hearts enlighten with thy ray,
    And kindle with thy love;
That, dead to earthly things, we may
    Live but to things above.

So when before the Judgment-seat
    The sinner hears his doom,
And when a voice divinely sweet
    Shall call the righteous home;

Safe from the black and fiery flood
    That sweeps the dread abyss,
May we behold the face of God
    In everlasting bliss.

To God the Father, with the Son,
    And Spirit evermore,
Be glory while the ages run,
    As in all time before.

LAUDS.

En clara vox redarguit.

HARK! an awful voice is sounding;
    "Christ is nigh!" it seems to say:
Cast away the dreams of darkness,
    "Oh ye children of the day!"

Startled at the solemn warning,
    Let the earth-bound soul arise;
Christ her Sun, all sloth dispelling,
    Shines upon the morning skies.

Lo! the Lamb so long expected,
    Comes with pardon down from Heaven;
Let us haste, with tears of sorrow,
    One and all to be forgiven.

So, when next He comes with glory,
    Wrapping all the earth in fear,
May He then as our Defender
    On the clouds of Heav'n appear.

Honour, glory, virtue, merit,
    To the Father and the Son,
With the co-eternal Spirit,
    While eternal ages run.

Christmas-Day.

VESPERS AND MATINS.

Jesu Redemptor omnium.

Jesu, Redeemer of the world!
  Before the earliest dawn of light
From everlasting ages born,
  Immense in glory as in might;

Immortal Hope of all mankind!
  In whom the Father's face we see;
Hear Thou the prayers thy people pour
  This day throughout the world to Thee.

Remember, O Creator Lord!
  That in the Virgin's sacred womb
Thou wast conceived, and of her flesh
  Didst our mortality assume.

This ever-blest recurring day
  Its witness bears, that all alone,
From thine own Father's bosom forth,
  To save the world Thou camest down.

O day! to which the seas and sky,
   And earth and Heav'n, glad welcome sing;
O Day! which heal'd our misery,
   And brought on earth salvation's King!

We too, O Lord, who have been cleansed
   In thy own fount of blood divine,
Offer the tribute of sweet song,
   On this dear natal day of thine.

O Jesus! born of Virgin bright,
   Immortal glory be to Thee;
Praise to the Father infinite,
   And Holy Ghost eternally.

LAUDS.

A solis ortus cardine.

From the far-blazing gate of morn
   To earth's remotest shore,
Let every tongue confess to Him
   Whom holy Mary bore.

Lo! the great Maker of the world,
    Lord of eternal years,
To save his creatures, veil'd beneath
    A creature's form appears.

A spotless maiden's virgin breast
    With heavenly grace He fills;
In her pure womb He is conceived,
    And there in secret dwells.

That bosom, chastity's sweet home,
    Becomes, oh, blest reward!
The shrine of Heav'n's immortal King,
    The temple of the Lord.

And Mary bears the babe, foretold
    By an Archangel's voice;
Whose presence made the Baptist leap,
    And in the womb rejoice.

A manger scantly strewn with hay
    Becomes th' Eternal's bed;
And He, who feeds each little bird,
    Himself with milk is fed.

Straightway with joy the Heav'ns are fill'd,
  The hosts angelic sing ;
And shepherds hasten to adore
  Their Shepherd and their King.

Praise to the Father! praise to Him,
  The Virgin's holy Son !
Praise to the Spirit Paraclete,
  While endless ages run !

The Holy Innocents.

MATINS.

Audit tyrannus anxius.

WHEN it reach'd the tyrant's ear,
  Brooding anxious all alone,
That the King of kings was near,
  Who should sit on David's throne ;

Stung with madness, straight he cries,
  " Treason threatens—draw the sword !
Rebels all around us rise !
  Drown the cradles deep in blood !"

What is guilty Herod's gain,
   Though a thousand babes he slay ?—
Christ, amid a thousand slain,
   Is in safety borne away.

Honour, glory, virtue, merit,
   Be to thee O Virgin's Son!
With the Father, and the Spirit,
   While eternal ages run.

LAUDS AND VESPERS.

Salvete flores martyrum.

Flowers of martyrdom all hail!
   Smitten by the tyrant foe
On life's threshold,—as the gale
   Strews the roses ere they blow.

First to bleed for Christ, sweet lambs!
   What a simple death ye died!
Sporting with your wreaths and palms,
   At the very altar side.

Honour, glory, virtue, merit,
　Be to Thee, O Virgin's Son!
With the Father and the Spirit,
　While eternal ages run.

Epiphany.

VESPERS AND MATINS.

Crudelis Herodes deum.

O cruel Herod! why thus fear
　Thy King and God, who comes below?
No earthly crown comes he to take,
　Who heavenly kingdoms doth bestow.

The wiser Magi see the star,
　And follow as it leads before;
By its pure ray they seek the Light,
　And with their gifts that Light adore.

Behold at length the heavenly Lamb
   Baptized in Jordan's sacred flood;
There consecrating by his touch
   Water to cleanse us in his blood.

But Cana saw her glorious Lord
   Begin His miracles divine;
When water, reddening at his word,
   Flow'd forth obedient in wine.

To Thee, O Jesus, who Thyself
   Hast to the Gentile world display'd,
Praise, with the Father evermore,
   And with the Holy Ghost, be paid.

LAUDS.

O sola magnarum urbium.

BETHLEHEM! of noblest cities
   None can once with thee compare;
Thou alone the Lord from Heaven
   Didst for us Incarnate bear.

Fairer than the sun at morning
　Was the star that told his birth;
To the lands their God announcing,
　Hid beneath a form of earth.

By its lambent beauty guided,
　See, the Eastern kings appear;
See them bend, their gifts to offer,—
　Gifts of incense, gold, and myrrh.

Solemn things of mystic meaning!—
　Incense doth the God disclose;
Gold a royal child proclaimeth;
　Myrrh a future tomb foreshews.

Holy Jesu! in thy brightness
　To the Gentile world display'd!
With the Father, and the Spirit,
　Praise eterne to Thee be paid.

Feast of the Most Holy Name of Jesus.

SECOND SUNDAY AFTER EPIPHANY.

VESPERS.

Jesu dulcis memoria.

Jesu! the very thought of Thee
    With sweetness fills my breast;
But sweeter far thy face to see,
    And in thy presence rest.

Nor voice can sing, nor heart can frame,
    Nor can the memory find,
A sweeter sound than thy blest name,
    O Saviour of mankind!

O hope of every contrite heart,
    O joy of all the meek,
To those who fall, how kind Thou art!
    How good to those who seek!

But what to those who find? ah! this
    Nor tongue nor pen can show :
The love of Jesus, what it is,
    None but his lovers know.

Jesu! our only joy be Thou,
    As Thou our prize wilt be ;
Jesu! be Thou our glory now,
    And through eternity.

MATINS.

[The same continued.]

Jesu Rex admirabilis.

O Jesu! King most wonderful!
    Thou Conqueror renown'd!
Thou Sweetness most ineffable!
    In whom all joys are found!

When once Thou visitest the heart,
    Then truth begins to shine ;
Then earthly vanities depart ;
    Then kindles love divine.

O Jesu! Light of all below!
　Thou Fount of life and fire!
Surpassing all the joys we know,
　And all we can desire.

May every heart confess thy name,
　And ever Thee adore;
And seeking Thee itself inflame,
　To seek Thee more and more.

Thee may our tongues for ever bless;
　Thee may we love alone;
And ever in our lives express
　The image of thine own.

LAUDS.

[The same continued.]

Jesu decus angelicum.

O Jesu! Thou the beauty art
　Of angel worlds above;
Thy name is music to the heart,
　Enchanting it with love.

Celestial sweetness unalloy'd!
    Who eat Thee hunger still;
Who drink of Thee still feel a void,
    Which nought but Thou can fill.

O my sweet Jesu! hear the sighs
    Which unto Thee I send;
To Thee mine inmost spirit cries,
    My being's hope and end!

Stay with us, Lord, and with thy light
    Illume the soul's abyss;
Scatter the darkness of our night,
    And fill the world with bliss.

O Jesu! spotless Virgin flower!
    Our life and joy! to Thee
Be praise, beatitude, and power,
    Through all eternity.

Friday after Septuagesima Sunday.

PRAYER OF OUR LORD JESUS CHRIST ON MOUNT OLIVET.

VESPERS AND MATINS.

Aspice ut Verbum Patris a supernis.

See from on high, array'd in truth and grace,
  The Father's Word descend!
Burning to heal the wounds of Adam's race,
  And our long evils end!

Pitying the miseries which with the Fall
  In Paradise began,
Prostrate upon the earth, the Lord of all
  Entreats for ruin'd man.

Oh, bitter then was our Redeemer's lot,
  While whelm'd in griefs unknown:
"Father," he cries, "remove this cup; yet not
  My will, but thine be done."

While, a dread anguish pressing down his heart,
  He faints upon the ground;
And from each bursting pore the blood-drops start,
  Moistening the earth around.

But quickly from high Heav'n an angel came,
  To soothe the Saviour's woes;
And strength returning to his languid frame,
  Up from the earth He rose.

Praise to the Father; praise, O Son! to Thee
  To whom a name is given
Above all names; praise to the Spirit be,
  From all in earth and Heaven.

LAUDS.

Venit e Cœlo Mediator a'to.

DAUGHTER of Sion! cease thy bitter tears,
  And calm thy breast;
Foretold through ages past, lo! now appears
  Thy Mediator blest.

That garden, where of old our guilt began,
    Wrought death and pain;
But this, where Jesus prays by night for man,
    Brings life and joy again.

Hither, of his own will, the Lord, for all
    Comes to atone;
And stays the thunderbolts about to fall
    From the dread Father's throne.

So shall He break the adamatine chain
    Of Hell's abyss;
And opening Heav'n long closed, call us again
    To his eternal bliss.

Praise to the Son, to whom a name above
    All names is given;
Praise to the Father and the Spirit of love,
    From all in earth and Heaven.

Friday after Sexagesima Sunday.

**THE PASSION
OF OUR LORD JESUS CHRIST.**

VESPERS.

Mœrentes oculi spargite lachrymas.

Now let us sit and weep,
And fill our hearts with woe;
Pondering the shame, and torments deep,
Which God from wicked men did undergo.

See! how the multitude,
With swords and staves, draw nigh;
See! how they smite with buffets rude
That head divine of awful majesty:

How, bound with cruel cord,
Christ to the scourge is given;
And ruffians lift their hands, unaw'd,
Against the King of kings and Lord of Heaven.

Hear it! ye people, hear!
Our good and gracious God,
Silent beneath the lash severe,
Stands with his sacred shoulders drench'd in blood.

O scene for tears! but now
The sinful race contrive
A torment new: deep in his brow,
With all their force the jagged thorns they drive.

Then roughly dragg'd to death,
Christ on the Cross is slain;
And, as He dies, with parting breath,
Into his Father's hands gives back his soul again.

To Him who so much bore,
To gain for sinners grace,
Be praise and glory evermore,
From the whole universal human race.

MATINS.

Aspice infami Deus ipse ligno.

See! where in shame the God of glory hangs,
    All bathed in his own blood:
See! how the nails pierce with a thousand pangs
    Those hands so good.

Th' All Holy, as a minister of ill,
    Betwixt two thieves they place;
Oh, deed unjust! yet such the cruel will
    Of Israel's race.

Pale grows his face, and fix'd his languid eye;
    His wearied head He bends;
And rich in merits, forth with one loud cry
    His Spirit sends.

O heart more hard than iron! not to weep
    At this; thy sin it was
That wrought his death; of all these torments deep
    Thou art the cause.

Praise, honour, glory be through endless time
    To th' everlasting God;
Who washed away our deadly stains of crime
    In his own Blood.

LAUDS.

Sævo dolorum turbine.

O'ERWHELM'D in depths of woe,
    Upon the Tree of scorn
Hangs the Redeemer of mankind,
    With racking anguish torn.

See! how the nails those hands
    And feet so tender rend;
See! down his face, and neck, and breast,
    His sacred Blood descend.

Hark! with what awful cry
    His Spirit takes its flight;
That cry, it smote his Mother's heart,
    And wrapt her soul in night.

Earth hears, and to its base
   Rocks wildly to and fro;
Tombs burst; seas, rivers, mountains quake;
   The veil is rent in two.

The sun withdraws his light;
   The midday heavens grow pale;
The moon, the stars, the universe,
   Their Maker's death bewail.

Shall man alone be mute?
   Come, youth! and hoary hairs!
Come, rich and poor! come, all mankind!
   And bathe those feet in tears.

Come! fall before His Cross,
   Who shed for us his blood;
Who died the victim of pure love,
   To make us sons of God.

Jesu! all praise to Thee,
   Our joy and endless rest!
Be Thou our guide while pilgrims here,
   Our crown amid the blest.

Friday after Quinquagesima Sunday.

**THE MOST HOLY CROWN OF THORNS
OF OUR LORD JESUS CHRIST.**

VESPERS AND MATINS.

Exite Sion filiæ.

Daughters of Sion! royal maids!
  Come forth to see the crown,
Which Sion's self, with cruel hands,
  Hath woven for her Son.

See! how amid his gory locks
  The jagged thorns appear;
See! how his pallid countenance
  Foretells that death is near.

Oh, savage was the earth that bore
  Those thorns so sharp and long!
Savage the hand that gather'd them
  To work this deadly wrong.

But now that Christ's redeeming Blood
   Hath tinged them with its dye,
Fairer than roses they appear,
   Or palms of victory.

Jesu! the thorns which pierced thy brow
   Sprang from the seed of sin;
Pluck ours, we pray thee, from our hearts,
   And plant thine own therein.

Praise, honour, to the Father be,
   And sole-begotten Son;
Praise to the spirit Paraclete,
   While endless ages run.

LAUDS.

Legis figuris pingitur.

CHRISTS'S peerless crown is pictured in
   The figures of the Law;—
The Ram entangled in the thorns;
   The Bush which Moses saw;

The Rainbow girding round the ark;
    The Table's crown of gold;
The Incense that in waving wreaths
    Around the Altar roll'd.

Hail Circlet dear! that didst the pangs
    Of dying Jesus feel;
Thou dost the brightest gems outshine,
    And all the stars excel.

Praise, honour, to the Father be,
    Praise to His only Son;
Praise to the blessed Paraclete,
    While endless ages run.

On Sundays and Week-days in Lent till Passion Sunday.

VESPERS.

Audi benigne Conditor.

Thou loving maker of mankind,
    Before thy throne we pray and weep;
Oh, strengthen us with grace divine,
    Duly this sacred Lent to keep.

Searcher of hearts! Thou dost discern
    Our ills, and all our weakness know:
Again to Thee with tears we turn;
    Again to us thy mercy show.

Much have we sinn'd; but we confess
    Our guilt, and all our faults deplore:
Oh, for the praise of thy great Name,
    Our fainting souls to health restore!

And grant us, while by fasts we strive
    This mortal body to control,
To fast from all the food of sin,
    And so to purify the soul.

Hear us, O Trinity thrice blest!
    Sole Unity! to Thee we cry:
Vouchsafe us from these fasts below
    To reap immortal fruit on high.

MATINS.

Ex more docti mystico.

Now with the slow-revolving year,
    Again the Fast we greet;
Which in its mystic circle moves
    Of forty days complete;

That Fast, by Law and Prophets taught,
    By Jesus Christ restored;
Jesus, of seasons and of times
    The Maker and the Lord.

Henceforth more sparing let us be
    Of food, of words, of sleep;
Henceforth beneath a stricter guard
    The roving senses keep.

And let us shun whatever things
    Distract the careless heart;
And let us shut our souls against
    The tyrant Tempter's art;

And weep before the Judge, and strive
   His vengeance to appease;
Saying to Him with contrite voice,
   Upon our bended knees:

Much have we sinn'd, O Lord! and still
   We sin each day we live;
Yet look in pity from on high,
   And of thy grace forgive.

Remember that we still are thine,
   Though of a fallen frame;
And take not from us in thy wrath
   The glory of thy name.

Undo past evil; grant us, O Lord,
   More grace to do aright;
So may we now and ever find
   Acceptance in thy sight.

Blest Trinity in Unity!
   Vouchsafe us, in thy love,
To gather from these fasts below
   Immortal fruit above.

LAUDS.

O Sol salutis intimis.

The darkness fleets, and joyful earth
   Welcomes the newborn day;
Jesu, true Sun of human souls!
   Shed in our souls thy ray.

Thou, who dost give the accepted time,
   Give tears to purify,
Give flames of love to burn our hearts
   As victims unto Thee.

That fountain, whence our sins have flow'd,
   Shall soon in tears distil,
If but thy penitential grace
   Subdue the stubborn will.

The day is near when all re-blooms,
   Thy own blest day, O Lord;
We too would joy, by thy right hand
   To Life's true path restored.

All glorious Trinity! to Thee
   Let earth's vast fabric bend;
And evermore from souls renew'd
   The Saints' new song ascend.

Friday after the first Sunday in Lent.

THE SPEAR AND NAILS OF OUR LORD JESUS CHRIST.

VESPERS.

Quænam lingua tibi, O Lancea, debitas.

WHAT tongue, illustrious Spear, can duly sound
   Thy praise, in heaven or earth?
Thou, who didst open that life-giving wound,
   From whence the Church had birth.

From Adam, sunk in an ecstatic sleep,
   Came Eve divinely framed;
From Christ, his spouse; when from that wound
   so deep
   The Blood and Water stream'd.

And equal thanks to you, blest Nails, whereby,
   Fast to the sacred Rood,
Was clenched the sentence dooming us to die,
   All blotted out in blood.

To Him who still retains in highest Heaven
   The wounds which here He bore,
Be glory, with th' eternal Father, given,
   And Spirit evermore.

MATINS.

Salvete Clavi et Lancea.

Hail, Spear and Nails! erewhile despised,
   As things of little worth;
Now crimson with the blood of Christ,
   And famed through Heav'n and earth.

Chosen by Jewish perfidy
   As instruments of sin,
God turn'd you into ministers
   Of love and grace divine:

For from each several wound ye made
  In that immortal frame,
As from a fount, celestial gifts
  And life eternal came.

Thee, Jesu, pierced with Nails and Spear,
  Let every knee adore;
With Thee, O Father, and with Thee,
  O Spirit, evermore.

LAUDS.

(The same continued.)

Tinctam ergo Christi sanguine.

Oh, turn those blessed points, all bathed
  In Christ's dear Blood, on me;
Mine were the sins that wrought his death,
  Mine be the penalty.

Pierce through my feet, my hands, my heart;
  So may some drop distil
Of Blood divine, into my soul,
  And all its evils heal.

So shall my feet be slow to sin,
  Harmless my hands shall be;
So from my wounded heart shall each
  Forbidden passion flee.

Thee, Jesu, pierced with Nails and Spear,
  Let every knee adore;
With Thee, O Father, and with Thee,
  O Spirit, evermore.

Friday after the second Sunday in Lent.

**THE MOST HOLY WINDING SHEET
OF OUR LORD JESUS CHRIST.**

VESPERS.

Gloriam sacræ celebremus omnes.

The glories of that sacred Winding-Sheet
  Let every tongue record;
Which from the Cross received with honour
    meet
  The body of the Lord.

O dear Memorial! on which we see,
  In bloody stains impress'd,
The form sublime in awful majesty,
  Of our Redeemer blest.

How doth the grievous sight of thee recall
  Those dying throes to mind,
Which Christ, compassionating Adam's fall,
  Endured for lost mankind!

His wounded side, his hands and feet pierced
  Mirror'd in thee appear;   [through
His lacerated limbs, his gory brow,
  And thorn-entangled hair.

Ah! who beholding these sad images,
  Can the big tears control?
Can check the throbs of swelling grief that rise
  Up from his inmost soul?

Jesu! my sin it was that laid Thee low,
  And through thy death I live;
That life, which to thy torments sore I owe,
  Henceforth to Thee I give.

Glory to him, who, to redeem us, bore
    Such bitter dying pains;
Who with th' eternal Father evermore,
    And Holy Spirit, reigns.

MATINS.

Mysterium mirabile.

THIS day the wondrous mystery
    Is set before our eyes,
Of Jesus stretch'd upon the Cross
    In dying agonies.

Oh, deed of love! the Prince becomes
    A victim for his slave;
The sinner an acquittal finds,
    The innocent a grave.

Whereof, in many a gory stain,
    The traces still are found
On yonder Winding-sheet, which wrapp'd
    The sacred body round.

Hail, trophies of our valiant Chief!
   Hail, proofs of triumph won
Over the World, and Hell, and Death,
   By God's Incarnate Son!

Be these the colours under which
   From this time forth we fight,
Against the cruel Serpent's guile,
   And all the powers of night.

So, dead to our old life, may we
   A better life begin;
And through the Cross of Christ at length
   Unto His Crown attain.

Father of mercies! hear our cry;
   Hear us, coequal Son!
Who reignest with the Holy Ghost
   While endless ages run.

LAUDS.

Jesu dulcis amor meus.

Jesu! as though Thyself wert here,
I draw in trembling sorrow near;
And hanging o'er thy form divine,
Kneel down to kiss these wounds of thine.

Ah me, how naked art Thou laid!
Bloodstain'd, distended, cold, and dead!
Joy of my soul—my Saviour sweet,
Upon this sacred Winding-sheet!

Hail, awful brow! hail, thorny wreath!
Hail, countenance now pale in death?
Whose glance but late so brightly blazed,
That Angels trembled as they gazed.

And hail to thee, my Saviour's side;
And hail to thee, thou wound so wide:
Thou wound more ruddy than the rose,
True antidote of all our woes!

Oh, by those sacred hands and feet
For me so mangled! I entreat,
My Jesu, turn me not away,
But let me here for ever stay.

Friday after the third Sunday in Lent.

**THE MOST HOLY FIVE WOUNDS
OF OUR LORD JESUS CHRIST.**

*Matins, Lauds, and Vespers, as on
Passion-Sunday.*

Friday after the fourth Sunday in Lent.

**THE MOST PRECIOUS BLOOD
OF OUR LORD JESUS CHRIST.**

VESPERS.

Festivis resonent compita vocibus.

Forth let the long procession stream,
 And through the streets in order wend ;
Let the bright waving line of torches gleam,
 The solemn chant ascend.

While we, with tears and sighs profound,
    That memorable Blood record,
Which, stretch'd on his hard Cross, from many
    The dying Jesus pour'd.   [a wound

By the first Adam's fatal sin
    Came death upon the human race;
In this new Adam doth new life begin,
    And everlasting grace.

For scarce the Father heard from Heaven
    The cry of his expiring Son,
When in that cry our sins were all forgiven,
    And boundless pardon won.

Henceforth, whoso in that dear Blood
    Washeth, shall lose his every stain;
And in immortal roseate beauty robed,
    An angel's likeness gain.

Only, run thou with courage on
    Straight to the goal set in the skies;
He, who assists thy course, will give thee soon
    Th' incomparable prize.

PROPER OF THE SEASON.

Father supreme! vouchsafe that we,
For whom thine only Son was slain,
And whom thy Holy Ghost doth sanctify,
May to thy joys attain.

MATINS.

Ira justa Conditoris.

HE who once, in righteous vengeance,
    Whelm'd the world beneath the flood,
Once again in mercy cleansed it
    With the stream of his own Blood,
Coming from his throne on high
On the painful Cross to die.

Blest with this all-saving shower,
    Earth her beauty straight resumed;
In the place of thorns and briers,
    Myrtles sprang, and roses bloom'd:
Bitter wormwood of the waste
Into honey changed its taste.

Scorpions ceased; the slimy serpent
    Laid his deadly poison by;
Savage beasts of cruel instinct
    Lost their wild ferocity;
Welcoming the gentle reign
Of the Lamb for sinners slain.

Oh, the wisdom of th' Eternal!
    Oh, its depth, and height divine!
Oh, the sweetness of that mercy
    Which in Jesus Christ doth shine!
Slaves we were condemned to die!
Our King pays the penalty!

When before the Judge we tremble,
    Conscious of his broken laws,
May this Blood, in that dread hour,
    Cry aloud, and plead our cause:
Bid our guilty terrors cease,
Be our pardon and our peace.

Prince and Author of Salvation!
   Lord of majesty supreme!
Jesu! praise to Thee be given
   By the world Thou didst redeem;
Who with the Father and the Spirit,
Reignest in eternal merit.

LAUDS.

Salvete Christi vulnera.

Hail wounds! which through eternal years
   The love of Jesus show;
Hail wounds! from whence unfailing streams
   Of grace and glory flow.

More precious than the gems of Ind,
   Than all the stars more fair;
Nor honeycomb, nor fragrant rose,
   Can once with you compare.

Through you is open'd to our souls
  A refuge safe and calm,
Whither no raging enemy
  Can reach to work us harm.

What countless stripes did Christ receive
  Naked in Pilate's hall!
From his torn flesh how red a shower
  Did all around Him fall!

How doth th' ensanguined thorny crown
  That beauteous brow transpierce!
How do the nails those hands and feet
  Contract with tortures fierce!

He bows his head, and forth at last
  His loving spirit soars;
Yet even after death his heart
  For us its tribute pours.

Beneath the wine-press of God's wrath
  His Blood for us He drains;
Till for Himself, O wondrous love!
  No single drop remains.

Oh, come all ye on whom abide
   The deadly stains of sin!
Come! wash in this encrimson'd tide,
   And ye shall be made clean.

Praise Him, who with the Father sits
   Enthroned upon the skies;
Whose Blood redeems our souls from guilt,
   Whose Spirit sanctifies.

Passion Sunday.

VESPERS.

Vexilla Regis prodeunt.

FORTH comes the Standard of the King:
   All hail, thou Mystery adored!
Hail, Cross! on which the Life Himself
   Died, and by death our life restored.

On which the Saviour's holy side,
   Rent open with a cruel spear,
Its stream of blood and water pour'd,
   To wash us from defilement clear.

O sacred Wood! fulfill'd in thee
    Was holy David's truthful lay;
Which told the world, that from a Tree
    The Lord should all the nations sway.

Most royally empurpled o'er,
    How beauteously thy stem doth shine!
How glorious was its lot to touch
    Those limbs so holy and divine!

Thrice blest, upon whose arms outstretch'd
    The Saviour of the world reclined;
Balance sublime! upon whose beam
    Was weigh'd the ransom of mankind.

Hail, Cross! thou only hope of man,
    Hail on this holy Passion-day!
To saints increase the grace they have;
    From sinners purge their guilt away.

Salvation's Fount, blest Trinity,
    Be praise to Thee through earth and skies:
Thou through the Cross the victory
    Dost give; oh give us too the prize!

MATINS.

Pange lingua gloriosi.

Sing, my tongue, the Saviour's glory ;
   Tell his triumph far and wide;
Tell aloud the famous story
   Of his Body crucified ;
How upon the Cross a Victim,
   Vanquishing in death, He died.

Eating of the Tree forbidden,
   Man had sunk in Satan's snare,
When his pitying Creator
   Did this second Tree prepare ;
Destined, many ages later,
   That first evil to repair.

Such the order God appointed
   When for sin He would atone;
To the Serpent thus opposing
   Schemes yet deeper than his own ;
Thence the remedy procuring,
   Whence the fatal wound had come.

So when now at length the fulness
   Of the sacred time drew nigh,
Then the Son who moulded all things
   Left his Father's throne on high;
From a Virgin's womb appearing,
   Clothed in our mortality.

All within a lowly manger,
   Lo, a tender babe He lies!
See his gentle Virgin mother
   Lull to sleep his infant cries!
While the limbs of God Incarnate
   Round with swathing-bands she ties.

Honour, blessing everlasting
   To th' immortal Deity!
To the Father, Son, and Spirit,
   Praise be pain coequally!
Glory through the earth and Heaven
   To Trinity in Unity!

LAUDS.

(The same continued.)

Lustra sex qui jam peregit.

Thus did Christ to perfect manhood
   In our mortal flesh attain:
Then of his free choice He goeth
   To a death of bitter pain;
And as a lamb, upon the altar
   Of the Cross, for us is slain.

Lo, with gall his thirst He quenches!
   See the thorns upon his brow!
Nails his tender flesh are rending!
   See, his side is open'd now!
Whence, to cleanse the whole creation,
   Streams of blood and water flow.

Lofty Tree, bend down thy branches,
   To embrace thy sacred load;
Oh, relax the native tension
   Of that all too rigid wood;
Gently, gently bear the members
   Of thy dying King and God.

Tree, which solely was found worthy
   Earth's great Victim to sustain;
Harbour from the raging tempest!
   Ark, that saved the world again!
Tree, with sacred Blood anointed.
   Of the Lamb for sinners slain.

Honour, blessing everlasting
   To the immortal Deity;
To the Father, Son, and Spirit,
   Praise be paid coequally!
Glory through the earth and Heaven
   To Trinity in Unity!

Low-Sunday, and through Easter to Ascension-day.

VESPERS.

Ad regias agni dapes.

Now at the Lamb's high royal feast
   In robes of saintly white we sing,
Through the Red Sea in safety brought
   By Jesus our immortal King.

O depth of love! for us He drains
   The chalice of his agony;
For us a Victim on the Cross
   He meekly lays Him down to die.

And as the avenging Angel pass'd
   Of old the blood besprinkled door;
As the cleft sea a passage gave,
   Then closed to whelm th' Egyptians o'er;

So Christ, our Paschal Sacrifice,
   Has brought us safe all perils through;
While for unleaven'd bread He asks
   But heart sincere and purpose true.

Hail, purest Victim Heav'n could find,
   The powers of Hell to overthrow!
Who didst the bonds of Death unbind;
   Who dost the prize of Life bestow.

Hail, victor Christ! hail, risen King
   To Thee alone belongs the crown;
Who hast the heavenly gates unbarr'd,
   And cast the Prince of darkness down.

O Jesu! from the death of sin
    Keep us, we pray; so shalt Thou be
The everlasting Paschal joy
    Of all the souls new-born in Thee.

To God the Father, with the Son
    Who from the grave immortal rose,
And Thee, O Paraclete, be praise,
    While age on endless ages flows.

MATINS.

Rex sempiterne cœlitum.

O Thou, the Heavens' eternal King
    Lord of the starry spheres!
Who with the Father equal art
    From everlasting years:

All praise to thy most holy Name,
    Who, when the world began,
Yoking the soul with clay, didst form
    In thine own image, Man.

And praise to Thee, who, when the Foe
    Had marr'd thy work sublime,
Clothing Thyself in flesh, didst mould
    Our race a second time;

When from the tomb new born, as from
    A Virgin born before,
Thou raising us from death with Thee
    Didst us in Thee restore.

Eternal Shepherd! who thy flock
    In thy pure Font dost lave,
Where souls are cleansed, and all their guilt
    Buried as in a grave;

Jesu! who to the Cross wast nail'd,
    Our hopeless debt to pay;
Jesu! who lavishly didst pour
    Thy blood for us away:

Oh, from the wretched death of sin
    Keep us; so shalt Thou be
The everlasting Paschal joy
    Of all new born in Thee.

To God the Father, with the Son
   Who from the grave arose,
And Thee, O Paraclete, be praise
   While age on ages flows.

LAUDS.

Aurora cœlum purpurat.

The dawn was purpling o'er the sky;
   With alleluias rang the air;
Earth held a glorious jubilee;
   Hell gnash'd its teeth in fierce despair:

When our most valiant mighty King
   From death's abyss, in dread array,
Led the long-prison'd Fathers forth,
   Into the beam of life and day:

When He, whom stone and seal and guard
   Had safely to the tomb consign'd,
Triumphant rose, and buried Death
   Deep in the grave He left behind.

"Calm all your grief, and still your tears;"
   Hark! the descending angel cries;
"For Christ is risen from the dead,
   And Death is slain, no more to rise."

O Jesu! from the death of sin
   Keep us, we pray; so shalt Thou be
The everlasting Paschal joy
   Of all the souls new born in Thee.

To God the Father, with the Son
   Who from the grave immortal rose,
And Thee, O Paraclete, be praise
   While age on endless ages flows.

The Ascension of our Lord.

VESPERS AND LAUDS.

Salutis humanæ Sator.

O Thou pure light of souls that love,
   True joy of every human breast,
Sower of life's immortal seed,
   Our Maker, and Redeemer blest!

What wondrous pity Thee o'ercame
   To make our guilty load thine own,
And sinless suffer death and shame,
   For our transgressions to atone

Thou, bursting Hades open wide,
   Didst all the captive souls unchain;
And thence to thy dread Father's side
   With glorious pomp ascend again.

O still may pity Thee compel
   To heal the wounds of which we die;
And take us in thy Light to dwell,
   Who for thy blissful Presence sigh.

Be Thou our guide, be thou our goal;
  Be Thou our pathway to the skies;
Our joy when sorrow fills the soul;
  In death our everlasting prize.

MATINS.

Æterne Rex altissime.

O Thou eternal King most high!
  Who didst the world redeem;
And conquering Death and Hell, receive
  A dignity supreme.

Thou, through the starry orbs, this day,
  Didst to thy throne ascend;
Thenceforth to reign in sovereign power
  And glory without end.

There, seated in thy majesty,
  To Thee submissive bow
The Heav'n of Heav'ns, the earth beneath,
  The realms of Hell below.

With trembling there the angels see
    The changed estate of men;
The flesh which sinn'd by Flesh redeem'd;
    Man in the Godhead reign.

There, waiting for thy faithful souls,
    Be Thou to us, O Lord!
Our joy of joys while here we stay,
    In Heav'n our great reward.

Renew our strength; our sins forgive;
    Our miseries efface;
And lift our souls aloft to Thee,
    By thy celestial grace.

So, when Thou shinest on the clouds,
    With thy angelic train,
May we be saved from deadly doom
    And our lost crowns regain.

To Christ returning gloriously
    With victory to Heaven,
Praise with the Father evermore
    And Holy Ghost be given.

Whit-Sunday.

VESPERS.

Veni Creator Spiritus.

Come, O Creator Spirit blest!
And in our souls take up thy rest;
Come, with thy grace and heavenly aid,
To fill the hearts which Thou hast made.

Great Paraclete! to Thee we cry:
O highest gift of God most high!
O fount of life! O fire of love!
And solemn Unction from above!

The sacred sevenfold grace is thine
Dread Finger of the hand divine!
The promise of the Father Thou!
Who dost the tongue with power endow.

Our senses touch with light and fire;
Our hearts with charity inspire;
And with endurance from on high
The weakness of our flesh supply.

Far back our enemy repel,
And let thy peace within us dwell,
So may we having Thee for guide
Turn from each hurtful thing aside.

O may thy grace on us bestow
The Father and the Son to know,
And evermore to hold confess'd
Thyself of Each the Spirit blest.

To God the Father praise be paid,
Praise to the Son who from the dead
Arose, and perfect praise to Thee
O Holy Ghost eternally.

MATINS.

Jam Christus astra ascenderat.

Above the starry spheres
 To where He was before
Christ had gone up, soon from on high
 The Father's gift to pour;

And now had fully come,
  On mystic cycle borne
Of seven times seven revolving days,
  The Pentecostal morn:

When, as the Apostles knelt
  At the third hour in prayer,
A sudden rushing sound proclaim'd
  The God of glory near.

Forthwith a tongue of fire
  Alights on every brow;
Each breast receives the Father's light,
  The Word's enkindling glow.

The Holy Ghost on all
  Is mightily outpoured;
Who straight in divers tongues declare
  The wonders of the Lord.

While strangers of all climes
  Flock round from far and near,
And with amazement, each at once
  Their native accents hear.

But faithless still, the Jews
  Deny the hand divine;
And madly jeer the saints of Christ,
  As drunk with new-made wine.

Till Peter in the midst
  Stood up, and spake aloud;
And their perfidious falsity
  By Joel's witness shew'd.

Praise to the Father be!
  Praise to the Son who rose!
Praise, Holy Paraclete, to Thee,
  While age on ages flows!

LAUDS.

Beata nobis gaudia.

AGAIN the slowly circling year
  Brings round the blessed hour,
When on the Saints the Paraclete
  Came down in grace and power.

In fashion of a fiery tongue
   On each and all He came;
Their lips with eloquence He strung,
   And fill'd their hearts with flame.

Straightway with divers tongues they speak,
   Instinct with grace divine;
While wond'ring crowds the cause mistake,
   And deem them drunk with wine.

These things were mystically wrought,
   The Paschal time complete,
When Israel's Law remission brought
   Of every legal debt.

God of all grace! to Thee we pray,
   To Thee adoring bend;
Into our hearts this sacred day
   Thy Spirit's fulness send.

Thou, who in ages past didst pour
   Thy graces from above,
Thy grace in us where lost restore,
   And 'stablish peace and love.

All glory to the Father be;
And to the Son who rose;
Glory, O Holy Ghost! to Thee,
While age on ages flows.

Trinity-Sunday.

VESPERS.

Jam Sol recedit igneus.

Now doth the fiery sun decline :—
Thou, Unity eternal! shine;
Thou, Trinity, thy blessings pour,
And make our hearts with love run o'er.

Thee in the hymns of morn we praise;
To Thee our voice at eve we raise;
Oh, grant us, with thy Saints on high,
Thee through all time to glorify.

Praise to the Father, with the Son,
And Holy Spirit, Three in One ;
As ever was in ages past,
And so shall be while ages last.

MATINS.

Summæ Parens clementiæ.

O Thou eternal Source of love!
   Ruler of Nature's scheme!
In Substance One, in Persons Three!
   Omniscient and Supreme!

Be nigh to us when we arise ;
   And, at the break of day,
With wakening body wake the soul,
   Her meed of praise to pay.

To God the Father glory be,
   And to th' eternal Son,
And Holy Ghost, coequally,
   While endless ages run.

LAUDS.

Tu Trinitatis Unitas.

O Thou! who dost all Nature sway,
   Dread Trinity in Unity!
Accept the trembling praise we pour
   To thy eternal Majesty.

The star that heraldeth the dawn
   Is slowly fading in the skies;
The darkness melts;—O Thou true light!
   Upon our darken'd souls arise.

To God the Father glory be,
   And to the sole-begotten Son;
And Holy Ghost coequally,
   While everlasting ages run.

Feast of Corpus Christi.
VESPERS.

Pange lingua gloriosi.

Sing, my tongue, the Saviour's glory,
   Of his Flesh the mystery sing;
Of the Blood, all price exceeding,
   Shed by our immortal King,
Destined, for the world's redemption,
   From a noble womb to spring.

Of a pure and spotless Virgin
   Born for us on earth below,
He, as Man with man conversing,
   Stay'd, the seeds of truth to sow;
Then He closed in solemn order
   Wondrously his life of woe.

On the night of that Last Supper,
   Seated with his chosen band,
He the Paschal victim eating,
   First fulfils the Law's command;
Then, as Food to his Apostles
   Gives Himself with his own hand.

Word made Flesh, the bread of Nature
   By his word to Flesh He turns ;
Wine into his Blood He changes :—
   What though sense no change discerns ?
Only be the heart in earnest,
   Faith her lesson quickly learns.

(Tantum ergo sacramentum.)

Down in adoration falling,
   Lo! the sacred Host we hail ;
Lo! o'er ancient forms departing,
   Newer rites of grace prevail ;
Faith, for all defects supplying,
   Where the feeble senses fail.

To the Everlasting Father,
   And the Son who reigns on high,
With the Holy Ghost proceeding
   Forth from Each eternally,
Be salvation, honour, blessing,
   Might, and endless majesty

MATINS.

Sacris solemniis juncta sint gaudia.

L<small>ET</small> old things pass away ;
  Let all be fresh and bright ;
And welcome we with hearts renew'd
  This feast of new delight.

Upon this hallow'd eve
  Christ with his brethren ate,
Obedient to the olden law,
  The Pasch before Him set.

Which done,—Himself entire,
  The true Incarnate God,
Alike on each, alike on all,
  His sacred hands bestow'd.

He gave his Flesh ; He gave
  His precious Blood ; and said,
"Receive, and drink ye all of this
  For your salvation shed."

Thus did the Lord appoint
This Sacrifice sublime,
And made his Priests its ministers
Through all the bounds of time.

Farewell to types! Henceforth
We feed on Angels' food:
The slave—oh, wonder!—eats the Flesh
Of his Incarnate God!

O Blessed Three in One!
Visit our hearts, we pray;
And lead us on through thine own paths
To thy eternal Day.

LAUDS.

Verbum supernum prodiens.

THE Word, descending from above,
  Though with the Father still on high,
Went forth upon his work of love,
  And soon to life's last eve drew nigh.

He shortly to a death accursed
   By a disciple shall be given;
But, to his twelve disciples, first
   He gives Himself, the Bread from Heaven.

Himself in either kind He gave:
   He gave his Flesh, He gave his Blood;
Of flesh and blood all men are made;
   And He of man would be the Food.

At birth our brother He became;
   At meat Himself as food He gives;
To ransom us He died in shame;
   As our reward, in bliss He lives.

(O salutaris Hostia.)

O SAVING Victim! opening wide
   The gate of Heav'n to man below!
Sore press our foes from every side;
   Thine aid supply, thy strength bestow.

To thy great Name be endless praise,
   Immortal Godhead, One in Three!
Oh, grant us endless length of days,
   In our true native land, with Thee!

𝔉riday after the 𝔒ctave of 𝔒orpus 𝔒hristi.

FEAST OF THE MOST SACRED HEART OF JESUS.

VESPERS.

Auctor beate sæculi.

Jesu, Creator of the world!
   Of all mankind Redeemer blest!
True God of God! in whom we see
   The Father's Image clear express'd!

Thee, Saviour, love alone constrain'd
   To make our mortal flesh thine own;
And as a second Adam come,
   For the first Adam to atone.

That selfsame love, which made the sky,
    Which made the sea, and stars, and earth,
Took pity on our misery,
    And broke the bondage of our birth.

O Jesu! in thy heart divine
    May that same love for ever glow;
For ever mercy to mankind
    From that exhaustless fountain flow.

For this, thy sacred heart was pierced,
    And both with blood and water ran;
To cleanse us from the stains of guilt,
    And be the hope and strength of man.

To God the Father, and the Son,
    All praise, and power, and glory be;
With Thee, O Spirit Paraclete,
    All through the long eternity.

MATINS.

En ut superba criminum.

Lo! how the savage crew
  Of our proud sins hath rent
The Heart of our all-gracious God,
  That Heart so innocent!

The soldier's quivering lance
  Our guilt it was that drave,
Our wicked deeds that to its point
  Such cruel sharpness gave.

O wounded Heart! whence sprang
  The Church, the Saviour's Bride;
Thou Door of our Salvation's Ark
  Set in its mystic side!

Thou holy Fount! whence flows
  The sacred sevenfold flood,
Where we our filthy robes may cleanse
  In the Lamb's saving blood:

By sorrowful relapse,
  Thee will we rend no more;
But like thy flames, those types of love,
  Strive Heavenward to soar.

Father and Son supreme!
  And Spirit! hear our cry;
Whose is the kingdom, praise and power,
  Through all eternity.

LAUDS.

Cor arca legem continens.

ARK of the Covenant! not that
  Whence bondage came of old;
But that of pure forgiving grace
  And mercies manifold.

Thou Veil of awful mystery!
   Thou Sanctuary sublime!
Thou sacred Temple, holier far
   Than that of olden time!

Blest Heart of Christ! in thy dear wound
   The hidden depth we see,
Of what were else unguess'd by us,—
   His boundless charity.

Beneath this emblem of pure love,
   'Twas Love Himself that died,
And offer'd up Himself for us,
   A Victim crucified.

Oh, who of his redeem'd will Him
   Their mutual love refuse?
Who would not rather in that heart,
   Their home eternal choose?

To God the Father, with the Son,
    And, Holy Ghost, to Thee,
Be honour, glory, virtue, power,
    Through all eternity.

Another Office of the same Feast.

VESPERS AND MATINS.

Quicunque certum quæritis.

ALL ye who seek a comfort sure
    In trouble and distress,
Whatever sorrow vex the mind,
    Or guilt the soul oppress:

Jesus, who gave Himself for you
    Upon the Cross to die,
Opens to you his sacred Heart,—
    Oh, to that heart draw nigh!

Ye hear how kindly He invites;
  Ye hear his words so blest;—
"All ye that labour, come to Me,
  And I will give you rest."

What meeker than the Saviour's Heart?—
  As on the Cross He lay,
It did his murderers forgive,
  And for their pardon pray.

O Heart! thou joy of Saints on high!
  Thou Hope of sinners here!
Attracted by those loving words,
  To Thee I lift my prayer.

Wash Thou my wounds in that dear Blood
  Which forth from Thee doth flow;
New grace, new hope inspire; a new
  And better heart bestow.

LAUDS.

Summi Parentis filio.

To Christ, the Prince of Peace,
   And Son of God most high,
The Father of the world to come.
   Sing we with holy joy.

Deep in his Heart for us
   The wound of love he bore;
That love, wherewith He still inflames
   The hearts that Him adore.

O Jesu! Victim blest
   What else but love divine,
Could Thee constrain to open thus
   That sacred Heart of thine?

O Fount of endless life!
   O Spring of waters clear!
O Flame celestial, cleansing all
   Who unto Thee draw near!

Hide me in thy dear Heart,
 For thither do I fly;
There seek thy grace through life, in death
 Thine immortality.

Praise to the Father be,
 And sole-begotten Son;
Praise, Holy Paraclete, to Thee,
 While endless ages run.

HYMNS FROM THE BREVIARY.

Part III.

HYMNS BELONGING TO THE PROPER OF SAINTS.

HYMNS FROM THE BREVIARY.

Part III.
HYMNS BELONGING TO THE PROPER OF SAINTS.

St. Peter's Chair at Rome.

January 18.

VESPERS AND MATINS.

Quodcunque in orbe nexibus revinxeris.

Peter, whatever thou shalt bind on earth,
  The same is bound above the starry sky;
What here thy delegated power doth loose,
  Is loosed in Heaven's supremest court on high
To judgment shalt thou come, when the world's
  end is nigh.

Praise to the Father, through all ages be;
  Praise to the consubstantial sovereign Son,
And Holy Ghost, One glorious Trinity;
  To whom all majesty and might belong;
So sing we now, and such be our eternal song.

LAUDS.

Beate Pastor Petre clemens accipe.

PETER, blest Shepherd! hearken to our cry,
  And with a word unloose our guilty chain;
Thou! who hast power to ope the gates on high
To men below, and power to shut them fast again.

Praise, blessing, majesty, through endless days,
  Be to the Trinity immortal given;
Who in pure Unity profoundly sways
Eternally alike all things in earth and Heaven.

Conversion of St. Paul the Apostle.

January 25.

VESPERS AND MATINS.

Egregie doctor Paule mores instrue.

LEAD us, great teacher Paul, in wisdom's ways,
 And lift our hearts with thine to Heaven's high throne;
Till Faith beholds the clear meridian blaze,
And sunlike in the soul reigns Charity alone.

Praise, blessing, majesty, through endless days,
 Be to the Trinity immortal given;
Who in pure Unity profoundly sways
Eternally all things alike in earth and Heaven.

St. Martina, Virgin and Martyr.
January 30.
VESPERS.

Martinæ celebri plaudite nomini.

Lift to the skies, great Rome, Martina's name,
Her triumph celebrate with glad accord;
Martina, high in merit, Virgin blest,
    And martyr of her Lord.

Beauty and youth, the joys of happy home,
Ancestral palaces, and noble birth;
All these were hers,—all these, for Jesu's sake
    She counted nothing worth.

Her wealth among the poor of Christ she shares
Intent on seeking better wealth above;
Herself she gives to her immortal King,
    Too happy in his love.

Expel false worldly joys; and fill us, Lord,
With thy irradiating beam divine;
Who with thy suffering martyrs present art,
    Great Godhead one and trine.

MATINS.

(The same continued.)

Non illam crucians ungula non feræ.

The agonizing hooks, the rending scourge,
Shook not the dauntless spirit in her breast;
With torments rack'd, Angels her fainting flesh
    Recruit with heavenly feast.

In vain they cast her to the ravening beasts;
Calm at her feet the lion crouches down:
Till smitten by the sword at length she goes
    To her immortal crown.

Now with the Saints Martina reigns in bliss;
And, where Idolatry sate throned of yore,
From her victorious altar praise and prayer
    With odorous incense soar.

Expel false worldly joys; and fill us, Lord,
With thy irradiating beam divine;
Who with thy suffering martyrs present art,
    Great Godhead one and trine.

LAUDS.

(The same continued.)

Tu natale solum protege, tu bonæ.

PROTECT thy native City, Spirit blest!
And give to Christendom sweet days of peace;
Bid the shrill trumpet, and the shock of war,
    Within her realms to cease.

And gathering her kings beneath the Cross,
Regain Jerusalem from our proud foe;
Avenge the innocent blood and the proud strength
    Of Islam overthrow.

O Pillar and defence of thine own Rome!
Her boast, her crown, her glory, and her praise!
This day thy memory she keeps;—accept
    The solemn rite she pays.

Expel false worldly joys; and fill us, Lord,
With thy irradiating beam divine;
Who with thy suffering martyrs present art,
    Great Godhead one and trine.

St. Gabriel the Archangel.
March 18.
VESPERS AND MATINS.

Christe, sanctorum decus angelorum.

O Christ! the beauty of the angel worlds!
Of man the Maker and Redeemer blest!
Grant us one day to reach those bright abodes
    And in thy glory rest.

Angel of Peace! thou, Michael, from above,
Come down, amid the homes of man to dwell;
And banish wars, with all their tears and blood,
    Back to their native Hell.

Angel of Strength! thou, Gabriel, cast out
Thine ancient foes, usurpers of thy reign;
The temples of thy triumph round the globe
    Revisit once again.

And Raphael, Physician of the soul,—
Let him descend from his pure halls of light,
To heal our sicknesses, and guide for us
    Each dubious course aright.

Thou too, fair virgin Daughter of the skies!
Mother of Light, and Queen of Peace! descend;
Bringing with thee the radiant Court of Heaven,
    To aid us and defend.

This grace on us bestow, O Father blest;
And thou, O Son by an eternal birth:
With Thee, from both proceeding, Holy Ghost,
    Whose glory fills the earth.

St. Joseph, Spouse of the Blessed Virgin Mary.

March 19.

VESPERS.

Te Joseph celebrent agmina cœlitum.

Joseph, pure Spouse of that immortal Bride,
Who shines in ever-virgin glory bright,
Through all the Christian climes thy praise be sung;
    Through all the realms of light.

Thee, when amazed concern for thy betrothed
Had fill'd thy righteous spirit with dismay,
An Angel visited, and, with blest words,
    Scatter'd thy fears away.

Thine arms embraced thy Maker newly born;
With Him to Egypt's desert didst thou flee;
Him in Jerusalem did seek and find;
    Oh grief, oh joy for thee!

Not until after death their blissful crown
Others obtain; but unto thee was given,
In thine own lifetime to enjoy thy God,
    As do the blest in Heaven.

Grant us great Trinity, for Joseph's sake,
Unto the starry mansions to attain;
There, with glad tongues, thy praise to celebrate
    In one eternal strain.

MATINS.

Cælitum Joseph decus atque nostræ.

Joseph! our certain hope below!
  Glory of earth and Heaven!
Thou Pillar of the world! to thee
  Be praise immortal given.

Thee, as Salvation's minister,
  The mighty Maker chose;
As Foster-father of the Word ;
  As Mary's spotless Spouse.

With joy thou sawest Him new born,
  Of whom the Prophets sang;
Him in a manger didst adore,
  From whom Creation sprang.

The Lord of lords, and King of kings,
  Ruler of sky and sea,
Whom Heaven, and Earth, and Hell obey,
  Was subject unto Thee.

Praise to the sacred Trine who Thee
  So glorifies on high,
And for Thy merits' sake may we
  Be sharers in Thy joy.

LAUDS.

Iste quem læti colimus fideles.

WORSHIPP'D throughout the Church to earth's
  far ends
With prayer and solemn rite,
Joseph this day triumphantly ascends
  Into the realms of light.

O, blest beyond the lot of mortal men!
  O'er whose last dying sigh,
Christ and the Virgin Mother watch'd serene,
  Soothing his agony.

Loosed from his fleshly chain, gently he fleets
  As in calm sleep away;
And diadem'd with light, enters the seats
  Of everlasting day.

There throned in pow'r, let us his loving aid
   With fervent prayers implore;
So may he gain us pardon in our need,
   And peace for evermore.

Glory and praise to Thee, blest Trinity!
   One only God and Lord,
Who to thy faithful ones unfailingly
   Their aureoles dost award.

Friday after Passion Sunday.

FEAST OF THE SEVEN DOLOURS OF THE BLESSED VIRGIN MARY.

VESPERS.

Stabat Mater dolorosa.

At the Cross her station keeping,
Stood the mournful Mother weeping,
   Close to Jesus to the last.

Through her heart, his sorrow sharing,
All his bitter anguish bearing,
  Now at length the sword had passed.

Oh, how sad and sore distress'd
Was that Mother highly blest
  Of the sole-begotten One!
Christ above in torment hangs;
She beneath beholds the pangs
  Of her dying glorious Son.

Is there one who would not weep
Whelm'd in miseries so deep
  Christ's dear Mother to behold?
Can the human heart refrain
From partaking in her pain,
  In that Mother's pain untold?

Bruised, derided, cursed, defiled,
She beheld her tender Child
  All with bloody scourges rent;

For the sins of his own nation,
Saw him hang in desolation,
  Till His Spirit forth He sent.

O thou Mother! fount of love!
Touch my spirit from above,
  Make my heart with thine accord:
Make me feel as thou hast felt;
Make my soul to glow and melt
  With the love of Christ my Lord.

MATINS.

(The same continued.)

Sancta Mater istud agas.

Holy Mother! pierce me through;
In my heart each wound renew
  Of my Saviour crucified:
Let me share with thee His pain,
Who for all my sins was slain,
  Who for me in torments died.

Let me mingle tears with thee,
Mourning Him who mourn'd for me.
All the days that I may live:
By the Cross with thee to stay;
There with thee to weep and pray;
Is all I ask of thee to give.

LAUDS.

(The same continued.)

Virgo virginum præclara.

VIRGIN of all virgins best!
Listen to my fond request:
Let me share thy grief divine;
Let me, to my latest breath,
In my body bear the death
Of that dying Son of thine.

Wounded with his every wound,
Steep my soul till it hath swoon'd
In His very blood away;

Be to me, O Virgin, nigh,
Lest in flames I burn and die,
  In His awful Judgment day.

Christ, when Thou shalt call me hence,
Be thy Mother my defence,
  Be Thy Cross my victory;
While my body here decays,
May my soul Thy goodness praise,
  Safe in Paradise with Thee.

St. Hermenegild, Martyr.

April 13.

VESPERS AND LAUDS.

Regali solio fortis Iberiæ.

GLORY of Iberia's throne!
  Joy of Martyr'd Saints above!
Who the crown of life have won,
  Dying for their Saviour's love:

What intrepid faith was thine
  In Thy every thought and deed!
Bent to do the will divine
  Wheresoever it might lead.

Every rising motion check'd
  Which might lead thy heart astray
How thou didst thy course direct
  Whither virtue shew'd the way.

Honour, glory, blessing, praise,
  To the Father and the Son,
With the Spirit, through all days,
  While eternal ages run.

MATINS.

(The same continued,)

Nullis te genitor blanditiis trahit.

From the Truth thy soul to turn,
  Pleads a Father's voice in vain;
Nought to thee were jewell'd crown,
  Earthly pleasure, earthly gain.

Angry threat and naked sword
  Daunted not Thy courage high;
Choosing glory with the Lord;
  Rather than a present joy.

Now amid the Saints in light,
  Throned in bliss for evermore;—
Oh! from thy exalted height,
  Hear the solemn prayer we pour.

Honour, glory, blessing, praise,
  To the Father and the Son,
With the Spirit, through all days,
  While eternal ages run.

The Apparition of St Michael the Archangel.

May 8.

VESPERS AND MATINS.

Te splendor et virtus Patris.

O JESU! life-spring of the soul!
   The Father's Power, and Glory bright!
Thee with the Angels we extol;
   From Thee they draw their life and light.

Thy thousand thousand hosts are spread,
   Embattled o'er the azure sky;
But Michael bears thy standard dread,
   And lifts the mighty Cross on high.

He in that Sign the rebel powers
   Did with their Dragon Prince expel;
And hurl'd them from the Heaven's high towers,
   Down like a thunderbolt to hell.

Grant us with Michael still, O Lord,
   Against the Prince of Pride to fight
So may a crown be our reward,
   Before the Lamb's pure throne of light.

To God the Father, and the Son,
  Who rose from death, all glory be;
With Thee, O blessed Paraclete,
  Henceforth through all eternity.

[*Within the Octave of the Ascension.*]

GLORY to Jesus, who returns
  In pomp triumphant to the sky,
To Thee, O Father, and with Thee,
  O Holy Ghost, eternally.

St. Venantius, Martyr.

May 18.

VESPERS.

Martyr Dei Venantius.

UNCONQUERED Martyr of his God!
  Camertium's light, her joy and prize
Venantius triumphs o'er his judge,
  And in victorious torment dies.

A boy in years,—when chains nor scourge
   Nor dungeon could his soul subdue ;
To lions with long hunger fierce
   At last the tender youth they threw.

But oh, what power hath innocence
   The fiercest nature to assuage !
The lions crouch to lick his feet,
   Forget their hunger and their rage.

Then downwards held in thickest smoke,
   They make him drink the stifling stream ;
While underneath slow torches sear
   His naked breast and side with flame

To Thee, O Father, with the Son,
   And Holy Spirit, glory be;
Oh, grant us, through thy Martyr's prayer,
   Pure joys of immortality.

MATINS.

Athleta Christi nobilis.

Noble Champion of the Lord!
Arm'd against idolatry!
In thy fervent zeal for God,
   Death had nought of fear for thee.

Bound with thongs, thy youthful form
   Down the rugged steep they tear;
Jagged rock and rending thorn
   All thy tender flesh lay bare.

Spent with toil, the savage crew
   Fainting sinks with deadly thirst:—
Thou the Cross dost sign; and lo!
   From the rock the waters burst.

Saintly Warrior Prince! who thus
   Thy tormentors couldst forgive;—
Shed the dew of grace on us,
   Bid our fainting spirits live.

Praise to Thee, dread Trinity,
  Father, Son, and Spirit blest!
Through thy Martyr's prayer may we
  Joys of life eternal taste.

LAUDS.

Dum nocte pulsa Lucifer.

The golden star of morn
  Is climbing in the sky;
The birth-day of Venantius
  Awakes the Church to joy.

His native land in depths
  Of Pagan darkness lay;
He o'er her guilty regions pour'd
  The dawn of Heavenly day;

When in the gracious stream
  He did her sons baptize,
Transmitting those who came to slay
  As martyrs to the skies.

With Angels now he shares
  Delights that never cease;—
Look down on us, O Spirit blest,
  And send us gifts of peace.

All honour, glory, praise,
  Blest Trinity, to Thee;
Oh, grant us through thy martyr's prayer
  Joys of eternity.

The Blessed Virgin Mary, the Help of Christians.

May 24.

VESPERS AND MATINS.

Sæpe dum Christi populus.

OFTTIMES, when hemm'd around by hostile arms,
The Christian people lay all sore dismay'd,
Faith's eye hath traced the Virgin gliding down,
  To lend her loving aid.

So speak the monuments of olden time,
And shrines that bright with votive spoils appear;
So speak the Festivals in her sweet praise,
    Returning year by year.

Now for new mercies a new song ascends,
While with our Lady's ensigns all unfurl'd,
Rome in procession long high triumph holds,
    And with great Rome the world.

Oh, happy day! on which Saint Peter's throne
Receives the Faith's great Ruler back again;
Returning from his banishment, in peace
    O'er Christendom to reign.

Ye youths and maidens, priests and people all
Pour out your grateful hearts on this glad day,
Striving with all your strength, to Heaven's high
    Her well-earned praise to pay.   [Queen.

Virgin of Virgins! Jesu's Mother blest!
Add yet another mercy to the past;
And help our Pastor all his flock to lead
    Safe into Heaven at last.

To Thee, great Trinity, be endless praise,
Blessing, and majesty, and glory due;
To Thee may we our hearts and voices raise,
All the long ages through.

LAUDS.

Te Redemptoris Dominique nostri.

MOTHER of our Lord and Saviour!
First in beauty as in power!
Glory of the Christian nations!
Ready help in trouble's hour!

Though the gates of Hell against us
With profoundest fury rage;
Though the ancient Foe assault us,
And his fiercest battle wage;

Nought can hurt the pure in spirit,
Who upon thine aid rely;
At thy hand secure of gaining
Strength and mercy from on high.

Safe beneath thy mighty shelter,—
  Though a thousand hosts combine,
All must fall or flee before us,
  Scatter'd by an arm divine.

Firm as once on holy Sion,
  David's tower rear'd its height;
With a glorious rampart girded,
  And with glistening armour bright:

So th' Almighty's Virgin Mother
  Stands in strength for evermore;
From Satanic hosts defending
  All who her defence implore.

Through the long unending ages,
  Blessed Trinity, to Thee;
Father, Son, and Holy Spirit!
  Praise and perfect glory be.

St. Juliana Falconieri, Virgin.
June 19.

VESPERS AND MATINS.

Cœlestis Agni nuptias.

To be the Lamb's celestial bride
  Is Juliana's one desire;
For this she quits her father's home,
  And leads the sacred virgin choir.

By day, by night, she mourns her Spouse
  Nail'd to the Cross, with ceaseless tears;
Till in herself, through very grief,
  The image of that Spouse appears.

Like Him, all Wounds, she kneels transfix'd
  Before the Virgin Mother's shrine;
And still the more she weeps, the more
  Mounts up the flame of love divine.

That love so deep the Lord repaid
  His handmaid on her dying bed;
When with the Food of heavenly life
  By miracle her soul He fed.

All glory, O Creator Sire,
   O sole-begotten Son divine,
And co-eternal Paraclete,
   One only Lord and God, be thine.

Nativity of St. John the Baptist.

June 24.

VESPERS.

Ut queant laxis resonare fibris.

UNLOOSE, great Baptist, our sin-fetter'd lips;
That with enfranchised voice we may proclaim
The miracles of thy transcendent life,
   Thy deeds of mighty fame!

Oh, lot sublime! an angel quits the skies,
Thy birth, thy name, thy glory to declare
Unto thy priestly sire: while to the Lord
   He offers Israel's prayer.

Mistrustful of the promise from on high,
His speech forsakes him at the angel's word;
But thou on thine eighth day dost re-attune
    For him the vocal chord.

No marvel; since yet cloister'd in the womb,
The presence of thy King had thee inspired;
What time Elizabeth and Mary sang,
    With joy prophetic fired.

Glory immortal to the Father be,
Praise to the sole-begotten sovereign Son,
With Thee, coequal Spirit, One in Three,
    While endless ages run,

MATINS.

(The same continued.)

Antra deserti teneris sub annis.

In caves of the lone wilderness thy youth
Thou hiddest, shunning the rude throng of men,
So the pure treasure of thy soul to guard
    From the least touch of sin.

There to thy sacred limbs the camel gave
A garment; the hard rock a bed supplied;
The stream thy thirst, locusts and honey wild
    Thy hunger satisfied.

Oh, blest beyond the Prophets of old time!
They of the Saviour sang that was to be:
Him present to announce, and show to all,
    Thy God reserved for thee!

Through the wide earth was never mortal man
Born holier than John; to whom was given
The guilty world's Baptizer to baptize,
    And ope the door of Heaven.

Glory immortal to the Father be,
Praise to the sole-begotten sovereign Son,
With Thee, coequal Spirit, One in Three,
    While endless ages run.

LAUDS.

O nimis felix meritique celsi.

O BLESSED Saint, of snow-white purity!
　　Dweller in wastes forlorn!
O mightiest of the Martyr host on high!
　　Greatest of Prophets born!

Of all the diadems that on the brows
　　Of Saints celestial shine,
Not one with brighter, purer, halo glows,
　　In Heaven's high Court, than thine.

Oh! then on us a tender, pitying gaze
　　Cast from thy glory's throne;
Straighten our crooked, smooth our rugged ways,
　　And break our hearts of stone.

So may the world's Redeemer find us meet
　　To offer Him a place,
Where He may deign to set his sacred feet,
　　Coming with gifts of grace.

Praise in the Heav'n to Thee, O First and Last,
　　The Trine eternal God!
Spare, Jesu, spare thy people, whom Thou hast
　　Redeem'd with thine own blood.

SS. Peter and Paul the Apostles.

June 29.

VESPERS.

Decora lux æternitatis auream.

Bathed in eternity's all-beauteous beam,
And opening into Heav'n a path sublime,
Welcome the golden day! that heralds in
The Apostolic Chiefs, whose glory fills all time!

Peter and Paul, the Fathers of great Rome!
Now sitting in the Senate of the skies!
One by the Cross the other by the Sword,
Sent to their thrones on high, and life's eternal
　　prize.

O happy Rome! whom that most glorious
   blood
For ever consecrates while ages flow;
Thou, thus empurpled, art more beautiful
Than all that doth appear most beautiful below.

Praise, blessing, majesty, through endless
   days,
Be to the Trinity immortal given;
Who, in pure Unity, profoundly sways
Eternally all things alike in earth and Heaven.

St. Elizabeth, Queen of Portugal,

July 8.

VESPERS AND MATINS.

Domare cordis impetus Elizabeth.

PURE, meek, with soul serene,
Sweeter to her it was to serve unseen
   Her God, than reign a queen.

Now far above our sight,
Enthroned upon the star-paved azure height,
  She reigns in realms of light;

So long as time shall flow,
Teaching to all who sit on thrones below,
  The good that power can do.

To God, the Sire and Son
And Paraclete, be glory, Trine in One,
  While endless ages run.

LAUDS.

Opes decusque regium reliqueras.

Riches and regal throne, for Christ's dear sake,
  True Saint, thou didst despise;
Amid the Angels seated now in bliss,
  Oh, help us from the skies!

Guide us; and fill our days with perfume sweet
  Of loving word and deed;
So teaches us thy beauteous charity
  By fragrant roses hid.

O charity! what power is thine! by thee
  Above the stars we soar;
In thee be purest praise to Father, Son,
  And Spirit, evermore.

St. Mary Magdalene.

July 22.

VESPERS.

Pater superni luminis.

FATHER of lights! one glance of Thine,
  Whose eyes the Universe control,
Fills Magdalene with holy love,
  And melts the ice within her soul.

Her precious ointment forth she brings,
: Upon those sacred feet to pour;
She washes them with burning tears;
: And with her hair she wipes them o'er.

Impassion'd to the Cross she clings;
: Nor fears beside the tomb to stay;
Nought of its ruffian guard she recks,
: For love has cast all fear away.

O Christ, thou very Love itself!
: Blest hope of man, through Thee forgiven
So touch our spirits from above,
: So purify our souls for Heaven.

To God the Father with the Son
: And Holy Paraclete, with thee,
As evermore hath been before,
: Be glory through eternity.

MATINS.

Maria castis osculis.

His sacred feet with tears of agony
She bathes; and prostrate on the ground
adores;
Steeps them in kisses chaste, and wipes them
dry
With her own hair; then forth her precious
ointment pours.

Praise in the highest to the Father be;
Praise to the mighty coeternal Son;
And praise, O Spirit Paraclete, to Thee,
While ages evermore of endless ages run.

LAUDS.

Summi Parentis Unice.

Son of the Highest! deign to cast
On us a pitying eye;
Thou, who repentant Magdalene
Didst call to endless joy.

Again the royal treasury
  Receives its long-lost coin;
The gem is found, and, cleansed from mire,
  Doth all the stars outshine.

O Jesu! balm of every wound!
  The sinner's only stay!
Wash Thou in Magdalene's pure tears
  Our guilty spots away.

Mother of God! the sons of Eve
  Weeping thine aid implore:
Oh! land us from the storms of life,
  Safe on th' eternal shore.

Glory, for graces manifold,
  To the one only Lord;
Whose mercy doth our souls forgive,
  Whose bounty doth reward.

St. Peter's Chains.

August 1.

VESPERS.

Miris modis repente liber ferrea.

THE Lord commands; and, lo, his iron chains,
   Falling from Peter, the behest obey:
Peter, blest shepherd! who, to verdant plains,
   And life's immortal springs, from day to day,
Leads on his tender charge, driving all wolves away.

Praise to the Father, through all ages be;
   Praise, blessing to the coeternal Son,
And Holy Ghost, One glorious Trinity;
   To whom all majesty and might belong;
So sing we now, and such be our eternal song.

The Transfiguration of our Lord Jesus Christ.

August 6.

VESPERS AND MATINS.

Quicunque Christum quæritis.

All ye who seek, in hope and love,
For your dear Lord, look up above!
Where, traced upon the azure sky,
Faith may a glorious form descry.

Lo! on the trembling verge of light
A something all divinely bright!
Immortal, infinite, sublime!
Older than chaos, space, or time!

Hail, Thou, the Gentiles' mighty Lord!
All hail, O Israel's King adored!
To Abraham sworn in ages past,
And to his seed while earth shall last.

To Thee the prophets witness bear;
Of Thee the Father doth declare,
That all who would his glory see,
Must hear and must believe in Thee.

To Jesus, from the proud conceal'd,
But evermore to babes reveal'd,
All glory with the Father be,
And Holy Ghost, eternally.

LAUDS.

Lux alma Jesu mentium.

Light of the soul, O Saviour blest!
Soon as Thy presence fills the breast,
Darkness and guilt are put to flight,
And all is sweetness and delight.

Son of the Father! Lord most high!
How glad is he who feels Thee nigh!
How sweet in Heaven Thy beam doth glow,
Denied to eye of flesh below!

O Light of Light celestial!
O Charity ineffable!
Come in Thy hidden majesty;
Fill us with love, fill us with Thee,

To Jesus, from the proud conceal'd,
But evermore to babes reveal'd,
All glory with the Father be,
And Holy Ghost, eternally.

Feast of the Seven Dolours of the Blessed Virgin Mary.

Third Sunday in September.

VESPERS.

O quot undis lachrymarum.

WHAT a sea of tears and sorrow
    Did the soul of Mary toss
To and fro upon its billows,
    While she wept her bitter loss;
In her arms her Jesus holding,
    Torn so newly from the Cross!

O that mournful Virgin Mother
  See her tears how fast they flow
Down upon his mangled body,
  Wounded side, and thorny brow;
While His hands and feet she kisses,—
  Picture of immortal woe!

Oft and oft His arms and bosom
  Fondly straining to her own;
Oft her pallid lips imprinting
  On each wound of her dear Son:
Till in one last kiss of anguish
  All her melting soul is gone.

Gentle Mother, we beseech thee,
  By thy tears and trouble sore;
By the death of thy dear Offspring;
  By the bloody wounds He bore;
Touch our hearts with that true sorrow
  Which afflicted Thee of yore.

To the Father everlasting,
   And the Son, who reigns on high,
With the coeternal Spirit,
   Trinity in Unity,
Be salvation, honour, blessing,
   Now and through eternity.

MATINS.

Jam toto subditus vesper eat polo.

Come, darkness, spread o'er Heaven thy pall,
   And hide, O sun, thy face;
While we that bitter death recall,
   With all its dire disgrace.

And thou, with tearful cheek, wast there;
   But with a heart of steel,
Mary, thou didst his moanings hear,
   And all his torments feel.

He hung before thee crucified ;
   His flesh with scourgings rent ;
His bloody gashes gaping wide ;
   His strength and spirit spent.

Thou his dishonour'd countenance,
   And racking thirst, didst see ;
By turns the gall, the sponge, the lance,
   Were agony to Thee.

Yet still erect in majesty,
   Thou didst the sight sustain ;—
Oh, more than Martyr ! not to die
   Amid such cruel pain !

Praise to the blessed Three in One ;
   And be that courage mine,
Which, sorrowing o'er her only Son,
   Did in the Virgin shine !

LAUDS.

Summæ Deus clementiæ.

God, in whom all grace doth dwell!
Grant us grace to ponder well
On the Virgin's Dolours seven;
On the wounds to Jesus given.

May the tears which Mary pour'd
Gain us pardon of the Lord;—
Tears excelling in their worth
All the penances of earth.

May the contemplation sore
Of the five wounds Jesus bore,
Source to us of blessings be,
Through a long eternity.

To the Incarnate Son who died
For His servants crucified,
Praise be render'd, with the Sire
And the Spirit Sanctifier.

Feast of the Most Holy Guardian Angels.

October 2.

VESPERS AND MATINS.

Custodes hominum psallimus angelos.

PRAISE we those ministers celestial
    Whom the dread father chose
To be defenders of our nature frail,
    Against our scheming foes.

For, since that from his glory in the skies
    Th' Apostate Angel fell,
Burning with envy, evermore he tries
    To drown our souls in Hell.

Then hither, watchful Spirit, bend thy wing,
    Our country's Guardian blest!
Avert her threatening ills; expel each thing
    That hindereth her rest.

Praise to the trinal Majesty, whose strength
    This mighty fabric sways;
Whose glory reigns beyond the utmost length
    Of everlasting days.

LAUDS.

Æterne Rector siderum.

RULER of the dread immense!
    Maker of this mighty frame!
Whose eternal Providence
    Guides it, as from Thee it came!

Prone before thy face we bend;
    Hear our supplicating cries;
And thy light celestial send,
    With the freshly dawning skies.

King of kings! and Lord most high
   This of thy dear love we pray,—
May Thy Guardian Angel nigh
   Keep us from all sin this day.

May He crush the deadly wiles
   Of the envious Serpent's art,
Ever spreading cunning toils
   Round about the thoughtless heart.

May he scatter ruthless war,
   Ere to this our land it come;
Plague and famine drive afar;
   Fix securely peace at home.

Father, Son, and Holy Ghost,
   One eternal Trinity!
Guard by thy Angelic Host
   Us, who put our trust in Thee.

Feast of the Maternity of the Blessed Virgin Mary.

Second Sunday in October.

MATINS.

Cælo Redemptor prætulit.

The Saviour left high Heaven to dwell
    Within the Virgin's womb;
And there array'd Himself in flesh.
    Our Victim to become.

She unto us divinely bore
    Salvation's King and God;
Who died for us upon the Cross,
    Who saves us in His blood:

She too our joyful hope shall be,
    And drive away all fears;
Offering for us to her dear Son
    Our contrite sighs and tears.

That Son—He hears His mother's prayer,
  And grants, ere it be said;
Be ours to love her, and invoke
  In every strait her aid.

Praise to the glorious Trinity,
  While endless times proceed;
Who in that bosom pure of stain
  Sow'd such immortal seed.

LAUDS.

Te Mater alma Numinis.

Mother of Almighty God!
  Suppliant at thy feet we pray;
Shelter us from Satan's fraud,
  Safe beneath thy wing this day.

'Twas by reason of our Fall,
  In our first Forefather's crime,
That the mighty Lord of all
  Raised Thee to thy rank sublime.

Oh then upon Adam's race
   Look thou with a pitying eye;
And entreat of Jesus grace,
   Till He lay his anger by.

Honour, glory, virtue, merit,
   Be to Thee, O Virgin's Son!
With the Father and the Spirit,
   While eternal ages run.

Feast of the Purity of the Blessed Virgin Mary.

Third Sunday in October.

VESPERS.

Præclara custos virginum.

BLEST Guardian of all virgin souls!
   Portal of bliss to man forgiven!
Pure Mother of Almighty God!
   Thou hope of earth, and joy of Heaven!

Fair Lily, found amid the thorns!
    Most beauteous Dove with wings of gold!
Rod from whose tender root upsprang
    That healing Flower long since foretold!

Thou Tower, against the dragon proof!
    Thou Star, to storm-toss'd voyagers dear!
Our course lies o'er a treacherous deep;
    Thine be the light by which we steer.

Scatter the mists that round us hang;
    Keep far the fatal shoals away;
And while through darkling waves we sweep
    Open a path to life and day.

O Jesu, born of Virgin bright!
    Immortal glory be to Thee;
Praise to the Father infinite,
    And Holy Ghost eternally.

MATINS.

O stella Jacob fulgida.

Star of Jacob, ever beaming
   With a radiance all divine!
'Mid the happy stars of Heaven
   Glows no purer ray than thine.

All in stoles of snowy brightness,
   Unto Thee the Angels sing;
Unto Thee the Virgin choirs,
   Mother of th' eternal King!

Joyful in Thy path they scatter
   Roses white and lilies fair;
Yet with thy chaste bosom's whiteness,
   Rose nor lily may compare.

Oh! that this low earth of ours,
   Answering th' angelic strain,
With Thy praises might re-echo,
   Till the Heavens replied again.

Honour, glory, virtue merit,
  Be to Thee, O Virgin's Son!
With the Father and the Spirit,
  While eternal ages run.

St. Teresa, Virgin.

October 15.

VESPERS AND LAUDS.

Regis superni nuntia.

Dear Herald of our King! thou didst
  Thy home in childhood leave;
Intending to barbaric lands
  Christ or thy blood to give.

But Thee a sweeter death awaits;
  A nobler fate is thine;
Pierced with a thousand heavenly darts,
  To die of love divine!

PROPER OF SAINTS.

Victim of perfect charity!
  Our souls with love inspire;
And save the nations of thy charge
  From everlasting fire.

Praise to the Father, with the Son,
  And Holy Spirit, be;
Praise to the blessed Three in One,
  Through all eternity.

MATINS.

Hæc est dies qua candidæ.

This day, beneath the form
  Of a pure snow-white dove,
Teresa's unbound Spirit sought
  The Sanctuary above:

And heard the Bridegroom's voice,—
  'Sister from Carmel come;
Come to the marriage of the Lamb,
  To thy eternal home.'

Spouse of the Virgin choir!
Let all the blest adore
Thee, Jesu! and in nuptial songs
Extol Thee evermore.

St. John Cantius, Confessor.

October 20.

VESPERS.

Gentis Polonæ gloria.

O GLORY and high boast
Of Poland's ancient race!
True father of thy fatherland!
True minister of grace!

'Twas thine the law of God
To preach, and to obey;
Oh, pray that we obedient be;
Nor from its precepts stray!

To th' Apostolic shrines
A pilgrim oft wast thou;
Oh guide aright, through this dark night,
Our pilgrimage below!

Thou to Jerusalem
Didst go for love, and there
The traces of thy Lord adore,
And wash with many a tear:

O sacred wounds of Christ!
Deep in our hearts remain!
May we through you the promise true
Of life eternal gain!

To Heaven's triunal Lord
Let the world's fabric bend;
While evermore, from hearts renew'd,
New hymns of praise ascend.

MATINS.

Corpus domas Jejuniis.

Thy body with long fastings worn;
Thy flesh with cruel scourgings torn;
'Twas thine to live, O blessed Saint,
A most unspotted penitent.

Oh, may we follow after thee,
In ways of holy purity!
And in the Spirit's might control
Each evil passion of the soul!

Thou to the poor in winter's snow
Oft thy own raiment didst bestow:
By hunger or by thirst oppress'd,
They flew to thy parental breast.

O thou, who nothing didst deny
To those who sought thy charity,
Thy native land from harm defend,
And peace on all her borders send!

Praise to the Father, with the Son,
And Holy Spirit, Three in One;
Jesu, through thy dear servant's prayer,
May we Thy joys eternal share.

LAUDS.

Te deprecante corporum.

SAINT of sweetest majesty!
    What a potent voice is thine!
At thy prayer diseases fly;
    Fading health revives again

Oft with wasting fever wan,
    Lingering at their latest breath,
Dying men by thee are drawn
    From the very jaws of death.

Oft the stores of golden grain,
    Hurried down the swollen flood,
At thy prayer return again
    Guided by the hand of God!

Such, O happy Saint in light,
  Such thy help in hour of need,
Oh, then from the heavenly height
  Harken now and intercede.

Everlasting Three in One!
  Everlasting One in Three!
Grant us through thy Saint the boon
  Of a blest eternity.

Feast of St. Raphael the Archangel.

October 25.

VESPERS AND MATINS.

Tibi Christe splendor Patris.

Jesu, brightness of the Father!
  Life and strength of all who live!
In the presence of the Angels,
  Glory to thy name we give;
And thy wondrous praise rehearse,
Singing in alternate verse.

Hail, all ye angelic Princedoms!
   Hail, ye thrones celestial!
Hail, Physician of Salvation!
   Guide of life, blest Raphael!
Binding fast the fiend of night,
In the glory of thy might.

Oh, may Christ beneath thy pinions
   Shield us from all harm this day;
Keep us pure in flesh and spirit;
   Save us from the enemy;
And vouchsafe us, of his grace,
In his Paradise a place.

Glory to th' Almighty Father,
   Sing we now in anthems sweet;
Glory to the great Redeemer;
   Glory to the Paraclete;
Godhead sole and Persons three!
In eternal unity!

LAUDS.

Christe, sanctorum decus angelorum.

O Christ, the glory of the Angel choirs!
Author and Ruler of the human race!
Grant us one day to climb the happy hills
    And see thy blissful face.

And oh, thy Raphael, physician blest,
Send down to us from you celestial height,
To heal our souls' diseases, and direct
    Our lifelong course aright.

Thou too, O Mary, Mother of our God!
And happy Queen of Angels! hither speed,
Drawing with thee the Army of the Saints
    To help us in our need.

This grace on us bestow, O Father blest,
And thou, O Son by an eternal birth;
With Thee, from both proceeding, Holy Ghost!
    Whose glory fills the earth.

Feast of All Saints.

November 1.

VESPERS AND MATINS.

Placare, Christe, servulis.

O Christ, thy guilty people spare!
   Lo, kneeling at thy gracious throne,
Thy Virgin Mother pours her prayer,
   Imploring pardon for her own.

Ye Angels, happy evermore!
   Who in your circles nine ascend,
As ye have guarded us before,
   So still from harm our steps defend.

Ye Prophets, and Apostles high!
   Behold our penitential tears;
And plead for us when death is nigh,
   And our all-searching Judge appears.

Ye Martyrs all! a purple band,
    And Confessors, a white-robed train;
Oh, call us to our native land,
    From this our exile, back again.

And ye, O choirs of Virgins chaste!
    Receive us to your seats on high;
With Hermits whom the desert waste
    Sent up of old into the sky.

Drive from the flock, O Spirits blest!
    The false and faithless race away;
That all within one fold may rest,
    Secure beneath one shepherd's sway.

To God the Father glory be,
    And to his sole-begotten Son;
And glory, Holy Ghost, to Thee,
    While everlasting ages run.

LAUDS.

Salutis æternæ dator.

Giver of life, eternal Lord!
  Thy own redeem'd defend;
Mother of Grace! thy children save,
  And help them to the end.

Ye thousand thousand Angel Hosts!
  Assist us in our need;
Ye Patriarchs! with the Prophet Choir!
  For our forgiveness plead.

Forerunner blest! and thou who still
  Dost Heaven's dread keys retain!
Ye glorious Apostles all!
  Unloose our guilty chain.

Army of Martyrs! holy Priests
  In beautiful array!
Ye happy troops of Virgins chaste!
  Wash all our stains away.

All ye who high above the stars
   In heavenly glory reign!
May we through your prevailing prayers
   Unto your joys attain.

Praise, honour, to the Father be,
   Praise to his only Son;
Praise, Holy Paraclete, to thee,
   While endless ages run.

HYMNS FROM THE BREVIARY.

Part IV.
HYMNS BELONGING TO THE COMMON OF SAINTS.

HYMNS FROM THE BREVIARY.

Part IV.

HYMNS BELONGING TO THE COMMON OF SAINTS.

Hymns on the Festivals of the Blessed Virgin Mary throughout the Year.

VESPERS.

Ave maris stella.

HAIL thou Star of ocean!
Portal of the sky!
Ever Virgin Mother
Of the Lord most High

Oh! by Gabriel's Ave,
   Utter'd long ago,
Eva's name reversing,
   'Stablish peace below.

Break the captive's fetters;
   Light on blindness pour;
All our ills expelling,
   Every bliss implore.

Shew thyself a Mother;
   Offer Him our sighs,
Who for us Incarnate
   Did not thee despise.

Virgin of all Virgins!
   To thy shelter take us;
Gentlest of the gentle!
   Chaste and gentle make us.

Still as on we journey,
   Help our weak endeavour;
Till with thee and Jesus
   We rejoice for ever.

Through the highest Heaven,
   To the Almighty Three,
Father, Son, and Spirit,
   One same glory be.

MATINS.

Quem terra, pontus, sidera.

THE Lord, whom earth, and air, and sea,
   With one adoring voice resound;
Who rules them all in majesty;
   In Mary's heart a cloister found.

Lo! in a humble Virgin's womb,
   O'ershadow'd by Almighty power;
He whom the stars, and sun, and moon,
   Each serve in their appointed hour.

O Mother blest! to whom was given
   Within thy compass to contain
The Architect of earth and Heaven,
   Whose hands the universe sustain:

To thee was sent an Angel down;
   In thee the Spirit was enshrined;
From thee came forth that Mighty One,
   The long-desired of all mankind.

O Jesu! born of Virgin bright,
   Immortal glory be to Thee;
Praise to the Father infinite,
   And Holy Ghost eternally.

LAUDS.

O gloriosa Virginum.

O Queen of all the Virgin choir!
   Enthroned above the starry sky!
Who with thy bosom's milk didst feed
   Thy own Creator Lord most high.

What man had lost in hapless Eve,
   Thy sacred womb to man restores;
Thou to the wretched here beneath
   Hast opened Heaven's eternal doors.

Hail, O refulgent Hall of light!
  Hail, Gate august of Heaven's high King!
Through Thee redeem'd to endless life,
  Thy praise let all the nations sing.

O Jesu! born of Virgin bright,
  Immortal glory be to Thee;
Praise to the Father infinite,
  And Holy Ghost eternally.

The above Hymns are also used in the Little Office *of the Blessed Virgin Mary, with the addition of the following:—*

AT TERCE, SEXT, NONE, AND COMPLINE.

Memento rerum Conditor.

REMEMBER, O Creator Lord!
  That in the Virgin's sacred womb
Thou wast conceived, and of her flesh
  Didst our mortality assume.

Mother of grace, O Mary blest!
  To thee, sweet fount of love, we fly;
Shield us through life, and take us hence
  To thy dear bosom when we die.

O Jesu! born of Virgin bright,
  Immortal glory be to Thee;
Praise to the Father infinite,
  And Holy Ghost eternally.

Common of Apostles and Evangelists.

VESPERS AND LAUDS.

Exultet orbis gaudiis.

Now let the earth with joy resound,
And Heaven the chant re-echo round;
Nor Heaven nor earth too high can raise
The great Apostles' glorious praise.

O ye who, throned in glory dread,
Shall judge the living and the dead!
Lights of the world for evermore!
To you the suppliant prayer we pour.

Ye closed the sacred gates on high;
At your command apart they fly:
Oh! loose for us the guilty chain
We strive to break, and strive in vain.

Sickness and health your voice obey;
At your command they go or stay:
From sin's disease our souls restore;
In good confirm us more and more.

So when the world is at its end,
And Christ to Judgment shall descend,
May we be called those joys to see
Prepared from all eternity.

Praise to the Father, with the Son,
And Holy Spirit, Three in One;
As ever was in ages past,
And so shall be while ages last.

MATINS.

Æterna Christi munera.

The Lord's eternal gifts,
   Th' Apostles' mighty praise,
Their victories, and high reward,
   Sing we in joyful lays.

Lords of the Churches they;
   Triumphant Chiefs of war;
Brave Soldiers of the Heavenly Camp;
   True lights for evermore.

Theirs' was the Saints' high Faith;
   And quenchless Hope's pure glow;
And perfect Charity which laid
   The world's fell tyrant low.

In them the Father shone;
   In them the Son o'ercame;
In them the Holy Spirit wrought,
   And fill'd their hearts with flame.

Praise to the Father, Son,
   And Spirit, One and Three;
As evermore, hath been before
   And shall for ever be.

Of Apostles and Evangelists during Easter.

VESPERS AND MATINS.

Tristes erant Apostoli.

When Christ, by his own servants slain,
   Had died upon the cruel Cross,
Th' Apostles of their joy bereft,
   Were weeping their dear Master's loss:

Meanwhile, an Angel at the tomb
   To holy women hath foretold,
'The faithful flock with joy shall soon
   Their Lord in Galilee behold.'

Who, as they run the news to bring,
   Lo, straightway Christ Himself they meet,
All radiant bright with heavenly light,
   And falling, clasp his sacred feet.

To Galilee's lone mountain height
   The Apostolic band retire:
There blest with their dear Saviour's sight,
   Enjoy in full their soul's desire.

O Jesu! from the death of sin
   Keep us, we pray; so shalt Thou be
The everlasting Paschal joy
   Of all the souls new-born in Thee.

To God the Father, with the Son,
   Who from the grave immortal rose;
And Thee, O Paraclete, be praise,
   While age on endless ages flows.

[**Within the Octave of the Ascension.**]

Glory to Jesus, who returns
 In pomp triumphant to the sky,
With Thee, O Father, and with Thee,
 O Holy Ghost, eternally.

LAUDS.

Paschale mundo gaudium.

Now daily shines the sun more fair,
 Recalling that blest time,
When Christ on his Apostles shone,
 In radiant light sublime.

They in his Body see the wounds
 Like stars divinely glow;
Then forth, as his true Witnesses,
 Throughout the world they go.

O Christ! thou King most merciful!
 Our inmost hearts possess;
So may our canticles of praise
 Thy name for ever bless.

Keep us, O Jesu! from the death
  Of sin; and deign to be
The everlasting Paschal joy
  Of all new-born in Thee.

Praise to the Father, and the Son,
  Who from the dead arose;
Praise to the blessed Paraclete,
  While age on ages flows.

Of one Martyr.

VESPERS AND MATINS.

Deus tuorum militum.

O Thou, of all thy warriors Lord,
Thyself the crown, and sure reward;
Set us from sinful fetters free,
Who sing thy Martyr's victory.

In selfish pleasures' worldly round
The taste of bitter gall he found;
But sweet to him was thy dear Name,
And so to heavenly joys he came.

Right manfully his cross he bore,
And ran his race of torments sore:
For Thee he poured his life away;
With Thee he lives in endless day.

We, then, before Thee bending low,
Intreat Thee, Lord, thy love to shew
On this the day thy Martyr died,
Who in thy Saints art glorified!

To God the Father, with the Son,
And Holy Spirit, Three in One,
Be praise and glory evermore,
As in th' eternity before!

LAUDS.

Invicte Martyr unicum.

MARTYR of unconquered might!
   Follower of th' Incarnate Son!
Who, victorious in the fight,
   Hast celestial glory won;

By the virtue of thy prayer,
   Let no evil hover nigh;
Sin's contagion drive afar;
   Waken drowsy lethargy.

Loosen'd from the fleshly chain
   Which detain'd thee here of old,
Loose us from the bonds of sin,
   From the fetters of the world.

Glory to the Father be:
   Glory to th' Incarnate Son;
Glory, Holy Ghost, to Thee,
   While eternal ages run.

The Common of one Martyr during Easter is the same as the above, except the Doxology, which is

Glory to th' Incarnate Son,
   Who from death immortal rose;
Glory to the Trine in One,
   While the flood of ages flows.

[**Within the Octave of the Ascension.**]

 Glory to th' eternal Son,
  Who again ascends the sky;
 Glory to the Trine in One,
  Through the long eternity.

Of many Martyrs.

VESPERS.

Sanctorum meritis inclyta gaudia.

Sing we the peerless deeds of martyr'd Saints,
Their glorious merits, and their portion blest;
Of all the conquerors this earth has seen,
  The greatest and the best.

Them in their day th' insensate world abhorred
They joyfully renounced it, Lord, for Thee;
Finding it all a barren waste, devoid
  Of fruit, or flower, or tree.

They trod beneath them every threat of man,
And came victorious all torments through;
The iron hooks, that piecemeal tore their flesh
    Could not their souls subdue.

Scourged, crucified, like sheep to slaughter led,
Unmurmuring they met their cruel fate;
For conscious innocence their souls upheld,
    In patient virtue great.

What tongue those joys, O Jesu, can disclose,
Which for thy martyred Saints Thou dost prepare!
Happy who in thy pains, thrice happy those
    Who in thy glory share!

Our faults, our sins, our miseries remove,
Great Deity supreme, immortal King!
Grant us thy peace, grant us thine endless love
    In endless life to sing.

MATINS.

Christo profusum sanguinem.

Sing we the Martyrs blest,
　Their blood for Jesus pour'd;
Sing we their glorious victories,
　And infinite reward.

Treading the world beneath,
　Spurning the body's pain,
'Twas theirs, in Martyrdom's brief space,
　Eternal joys to gain.

Consign'd to raging flames
　Or ruthless beasts a prey;
Their tender flesh by savage hooks
　Torn piece by piece away;

Their vitals hanging forth;
　Unmoved they still endure;
Unmoved continue, in the grace
　Of endless life secure.

Saviour, to us vouchsafe,
Of thy dear clemency,
A portion with thy Martyr Saints,
Through all eternity,

LAUDS.

Rex gloriose martyrum.

O Thou, the Martyrs' glorious King!
Of Confessors the crown and prize;
Who dost to joy celestial bring
Those who the joys of earth despise;

By all the praise thy Saints have won;
By all their pains in days gone by;
By all the deeds which they have done;
Hear Thou thy suppliant people's cry.

Thou dost amid thy Martyrs fight;
Thy Confessors Thou dost forgive;
May we find mercy in thy sight,
And in thy sacred presence live.

To God the Father glory be,
 And to his sole-begotten Son;
And glory, Holy Ghost, to Thee !
 While everlasting ages run.

Of many Martyrs during Easter Time.

VESPERS AND LAUDS.

Rex gloriose martyrum.

As above, page 214.

With the following Doxology.

Now to the Father, and the Son,
 Who rose from death, all glory be,
With Thee, O holy Comforter,
 Henceforth through all eternity.

MATINS.

Christo profusum sanguinem.

As at page 213.

Of a Confessor and Bishop.

VESPERS AND MATINS.

Iste Confessor Domini colentes.

The Confessor of Christ, from shore to shore
    Worshipped with solemn rite;
This day with merits full, his labours o'er,
    Went to his seat in light.

[If it be not the day of his death, the following
is substituted.]

This day receives those honours which are his,
    High in the realms of light.

Holy and innocent were all his ways;
    Sweet, temperate, unstain'd;
His life was prayer,—his every breath was praise,
    While breath to him remain'd.

Ofttimes have miracles in many a land
    His sanctity display'd;
And still does health return at his command
    To many a frame decay'd.

Therefore to him triumphant praise we pay,
    And yearly songs renew ;
Praying our glorious Saint for us to pray,
    All the long ages through.

To God, of all the centre and the source,
    Be power and glory given;
Who sways the mighty world through all its course,
    From the bright throne of Heaven.

LAUDS.

Jesu Redemptor omnium.

REDEEMER blest of all who live !
    Thy Pontiffs' endless prize !
Upon this day thine ear incline,
    And hear us from the skies.

This day the holy Confessor
    Of thy most sacred Name,
Honour'd with yearly festive rites,
    To heavenly glory came.

This day amid the blissful choirs
  Of Angels, he sate down;
Receiving, for the joys he spurn'd,
  An everlasting crown.

Oh! grant us in his steps to walk;
  His holy life to live;
And by the virtue of his prayers,
  Thy people's sins forgive.

Glory to Thee, O Lord and Christ;
  Praise to the Father be;
Praise to the Spirit Paraclete;
  Through all eternity.

Of a Confessor not a Bishop.

VESPERS AND MATINS.

Iste Confessor.

As at page 216.

LAUDS.

Jesu corona celsior.

Jesu! eternal Truth sublime!
   Through endless years the same!
Thou crown of those who through all time
   Confess thy holy Name:

Thy suppliant people, through the prayer
   Of thy blest Saint, forgive;
For his dear sake, thy wrath forbear,
   And bid our spirits live.

Again returns the sacred day,
   With heavenly glory bright,
Which saw him go upon his way
   Into the realms of light.

All objects of our vain desire,
   All earthly joys and gains,
To him were but as filthy mire;
   And now with Thee he reigns.

Thee, Jesu, his all-gracious Lord,
  Confessing to the last,
He trod beneath him Satan's fraud,
  And stood for ever fast.

In holy deeds of faith and love,
  In fastings and in prayers,
His days were spent; and now above
  Thy heavenly Feast he shares.

Then, for his sake thy wrath lay by,
  And hear us while we pray;
And pardon us, O Thou most high,
  On this his festal Day.

All glory to the Father be;
  And sole Incarnate Son;
Praise, holy Paraclete, to Thee;
  While endless ages run.

Of Virgins.

VESPERS AND LAUDS.

Jesu corona Virginum.

DEAR Crown of all the Virgin choir!
    That holy Mother's Virgin Son!
Who is, alone of womankind,
    Mother and Virgin both in one.

Encircled by thy virgin band,
    Amid the lilies Thou art found;
For thy pure brides with lavish hand
    Scattering immortal graces round.

And still wherever thou dost bend
    Thy lovely steps, O glorious King,
Virgins upon thy steps attend,
    And hymns to thy high glory sing.

Keep us, O Purity divine,
    From every least corruption free;
Our every sense from sin refine,
    And purify our souls for Thee.

To God the Father, and the Son,
   All honour, glory, praise, be given;
With Thee, coequal Paraclete!
   For evermore in earth and Heaven.

MATINS.

Virginis Proles Opifexque matris.

O Thou thy Mother's Maker, hail!
   Hail, Virgin-born! to Thee;
To-day a Virgin's death we sing,
   A Virgin's victory.

O doubly blest! to whom was given
   Martyr and Virgin too,—
At once to triumph over death,
   And her frail sex subdue.

O'er fear, o'er thousand forms of pain,
   Victorious she stood;
And won the blissful heavenly heights
   In streams of her own blood.

Oh, through her prayers our sins forgive,
  All good and gracious King!
So may we purified in heart
  Thy praise eternal sing.

All glory to the Father be;
  And sole begotten Son;
With Thee, who dost from both proceed,
  While endless ages run.

[If the Virgin be not a Martyr, the second and third stanzas are omitted, and the two last lines of the first stanza are as follows.]

Look down in love on us who keep
  Thy Virgin's memory.

Of Holy Women.

VESPERS AND LAUDS.

Fortem virili pectore.

LAUD we the Saint most sweet
Shining in glory blest,
Who bore a hero's noble heart
Within a woman's breast.

Pierced with the love of Christ
The world's false love she fled;
And Heavenward with might and main
Upon her journey sped.

With fasts she pined the flesh,
But on sweet food of prayer
Feasted her spirit pure; and now
Doth joys eternal share.

O Christ our King and God!
Thou strength of all the strong!
To whom alone all holy deeds,
And all great works belong;

For her dear plaints on high,
To us propitious be;
And in the glorious Trinity
Glory eterne to Thee.

MATINS.

" Oh, through her prayers," &c., p. 223.

Of the Dedication of a Church.

VESPERS AND MATINS.

Cœlestis urbs Jerusalem.

JERUSALEM, thou City blest!
Dear vision of celestial rest!
Which far above the starry sky,
Piled up with living stones on high,
Art, as a Bride, encircled bright,
With million angel forms of light:

Oh, wedded in a prosperous hour!
The Father's glory was thy dower;
The Spirit all His graces shed,
Thou peerless Queen, upon thy head;
When Christ espoused thee for his Bride,
O City bright and glorified!

Thy gates a pearly lustre pour;
Thy gates are open evermore;
And thither evermore draw nigh
All who for Christ have dared to die;
Or smit with love of their dear Lord,
Have pains endured and joys abhorr'd.

Type of the Church which here we see,
Oh what a task hath builded thee!
Long did the chisels ring around!
Long did the mallets' blows rebound!
Long work'd the head, and toil'd the hand!
Ere stood thy stones as now they stand!

To God the Father, glory due
Be paid by all the heavenly Host;
And to His only Son most true;
With Thee, O mighty Holy Ghost!
To whom praise, pow'r, and blessing be,
Through th' ages of eternity.

LAUDS.

Alto ex Olympi vertice.

From highest Heav'n, the Father's Son,
Descending like that mystic stone
Cut from a mountain without hands,
Came down below, and fill'd all lands;
Uniting, midway in the sky,
His House on earth, and House on high.

That House on high,—it ever rings
With praises of the King of kings;
For ever there, on harps divine,
They hymn th' eternal One and Trine;
We, here below, the strain prolong,
And faintly echo Sion's song.

O Lord of lords invisible!
With thy pure light this temple fill:
Hither, oft as invoked, descend;
Here to thy people's prayer attend;
Here, through all hearts, for evermore,
Thy Spirit's quick'ning graces pour.

Here may the Faithful, day by day,
Their hearts' adoring homage pay;
And here receive from thy dear love
The blessings of that home above;
Till loosen'd from this mortal chain,
Its everlasting joys they gain.

To God the Father, glory due
Be paid by all the heavenly Host;
And to His only Son most true;
With Thee, O mighty Holy Ghost!
To whom praise, pow'r, and blessing be,
Through th' ages of eternity.

END OF HYMNS FROM THE BREVIARY.

HYMNS FROM THE MISSAL.

HYMNS FROM THE MISSAL.

Palm-Sunday.

Gloria, laus, et honor.

GLORY and praise to Thee, Redeemer blest,
Whom children with hosannas glad confess'd !
   Glory and praise, &c.; *is repeated.*

Hail, Israel's King ! hail, David's Son adored,
Who comest in the name of Israel's Lord !
   Glory and praise, &c.

Thy praise in Heav'n the host angelic sings ;
On earth mankind, with all created things.
   Glory and praise, &c.

Thee with their palms the Jews went forth to meet;
Thee now with prayers and holy hymns we greet.

> Glory and praise, &c.

Thee, on thy way to die, they crown'd with praise;
To Thee, now King on high, our song we raise.

> Glory and praise, &c.

Their poor homage pleased Thee, good and gracious King!
Ours too accept,—the best that we can bring.

> Glory and praise, &c.

Good-Friday.

Crux fidelis inter omnes.

FAITHFUL Cross, O Tree all beauteous!
   Tree all peerless and divine!
Not a grove on earth can show us
   Such a leaf and flower as thine.
Sweet the nails, and sweet the wood,
Laden with so sweet a load!

After which, "*Pange lingua,*" as at page 91.

["Sweet the nails," &c. *as above, being repeated after every stanza.*]

Sequence, Easter-Sunday.

Victimæ Paschali laudes.

FORTH to the paschal Victim, Christians, bring
   Your sacrifice of praise:

The Lamb redeems the sheep;
   And Christ, the Sinless One,
   Hath to the Father sinners reconciled.

Together Death and Life
    In a strange conflict strove;
    The Prince of Life, who died,
    Now lives and reigns.

What thou sawest, Mary, say,
    As thou wentest on the way.

I saw the tomb wherein the Living One had lain
I saw His glory as He rose again;
Napkin and linen clothes, and Angels twain;
    Yea, Christ is risen, my hope, and He
    Will go before you into Galilee.

We know that Christ indeed has risen from the
    Hail, thou King of Victory!   [grave:
Have mercy, Lord, and save.

Sequence, Whit-Sunday.

Veni Sancte Spiritus.

HOLY Spirit! Lord of light!
From thy clear celestial height
    Thy pure beaming radiance give:

Come, Thou Father of the poor!
Come, with treasures which endure!
  Come, Thou Light of all that live!

Thou, of all consolers best,
Thou the soul's delightsome guest,
  Dost refreshing peace bestow;

Thou in toil art comfort sweet;
Pleasant coolness in the heat;
  Solace in the midst of woe.

Light immortal! light divine!
Visit Thou these hearts of thine,
  And our inmost being fill:

If Thou take thy grace away,
Nothing pure in man will stay;
  All his good is turned to ill.

Heal our wounds; our strength renew;
On our dryness pour thy dew;
  Wash the stains of guilt away:

Bend the stubborn heart and will;
Melt the frozen, warm the chill;
  Guide the steps that go astray.

Thou, on those who evermore
Thee confess and Thee adore,
  In thy sevenfold gifts, descend:

Give them comfort when they die;
Give them life with Thee on high;
  Give them joys that never end.

Sequence, Solemnity of Corpus Christi.

Lauda Sion Salvatorem.

Sion, lift thy voice, and sing;
Praise thy Saviour and thy King;
  Praise with hymns thy Shepherd true:
Dare thy most to praise Him well;
For He doth all praise excel;
  None can ever reach His due.

Special theme of praise is thine,
That true living Bread divine,
　That life-giving Flesh adored,
Which the brethren twelve received,
As most faithfully believed,
　At the Supper of the Lord.

Let the chant be loud and high;
Sweet and tranquil be the joy
　Felt to-day in every breast;
On this Festival divine
Which recounts the origin
　Of the glorious Eucharist.

At this Table of the King,
Our new Paschal offering
　Brings to end the olden rite;
Here, for empty shadows fled,
Is Reality instead;
　Here, instead of darkness, Light.

His own act, at supper seated,
Christ ordain'd to be repeated,
  In His Memory divine;
Wherefore now, with adoration,
We the Host of our salvation
  Consecrate from bread and wine.

Hear what holy Church maintaineth,
That the bread its substance changeth
  Into Flesh, the wine to Blood.
Doth it pass thy comprehending?
Faith, the law of sight transcending,
  Leaps to things not understood.

Here, in outward signs are hidden
Priceless things, to sense forbidden;
  Signs, not things, are all we see;—
Flesh from bread, and Blood from wine;
Yet is Christ, in either sign,
  All entire, confess'd to be.

They too, who of Him partake,
Sever not, nor rend, nor break,
   But entire, their Lord receive.
Whether one or thousands eat,
All receive the self-same meat,
   Nor the less for others leave.

Both the wicked and the good
Eat of this celestial Food;
   But with ends how opposite!
Here 'tis life; and there 'tis death;
The same, yet issuing to each
   In a difference infinite.

Nor a single doubt retain,
When they break the Host in twain,
But that in each part remains
   What was in the whole before;
Since the simple sign alone
Suffers change in state or form,
The Signified remaining One
   And the Same for evermore.

[Ecce panis angelorum.]

Lo! upon the Altar lies,
Hidden deep from human eyes,
Angels' Bread from Paradise,
  Made the food of mortal man :
Children's meat to dogs denied ;
In old types foresignified ;
In the manna from the skies,
  In Isaac, and the Paschal Lamb.

Jesu ! Shepherd of the sheep !
Thy true flock in safety keep.
Living Bread! thy life supply;
Strengthen us, or else we die;
  Fill us with celestial grace :
Thou, who feedest us below !
Source of all we have or know !
Grant that with thy Saints above,
Sitting at the feast of love,
  We may see Thee face to face,

Sequence, Mass for the Dead.

Dies iræ dies illa.

Nigher still, and still more nigh
Draws the Day of Prophecy,
That dissolveth earth and sky.

Oh, what trembling there shall be,
When the world its Judge shall see,
Coming in dread majesty!

Hark! the trump, with thrilling tone,
From sepulchral regions lone,
Summons all before the throne:

Time and Death it doth appal,
To see the buried ages all
Rise to answer at the call.

Now the books are open spread;
Now the writing must be read,
Which arraigns the quick and dead:

Now, before the Judge severe
Hidden things must all appear;
Nought can pass unpunish'd here.

What shall guilty I then plead?
Who for me will intercede,
When the Saints shall comfort need?

King of dreadful Majesty!
Who dost freely justify!
Fount of Pity, save Thou me!

Recollect, O Love divine!
'Twas for this lost sheep of thine
Thou thy glory didst resign:

Satest wearied seeking me;
Sufferedst upon the Tree:
Let not vain thy labour be.

Judge of Justice, hear my prayer!
Spare me, Lord, in mercy spare!
Ere the Reckoning-day appear.

Lo! thy gracious face I seek;
Shame and grief are on my cheek;
Sighs and tears my sorrow speak.

Thou didst Mary's guilt forgive;
Didst the dying thief receive;
Hence doth hope within me live.

Worthless are my prayers, I know;
Yet, oh, cause me not to go
Into fire of endless woe.

Sever'd from the guilty band,
Make me with thy sheep to stand,
Placing me on thy right hand.

When the cursed in anguish flee
Into flames of misery;
With the Blest then call Thou me.

Suppliant in the dust I lie;
My heart a cinder, crush'd and dry;
Help me, Lord, when death is nigh!

Full of tears, and full of dread,
Is the day that wakes the dead,
Calling all, with solemn blast,
From the ashes of the past.

Lord of mercy! Jesu blest!
Grant the Faithful light and rest.

For *Stabat Mater dolorosa,* see page 138.

HYMNS FROM VARIOUS SOURCES.

HYMNS FROM VARIOUS SOURCES.

HYMNS AT
BENEDICTION OF THE BLESSED SACRAMENT.

Rhyme of St. Thomas Aquinas.

Adora Te devote latens Deitas.

O GODHEAD hid, devoutly I adore Thee,
Who truly art within the forms before me
To Thee my heart I bow with bended knee,
As failing quite in contemplating Thee.

Sight, touch, and taste in Thee are each deceived;
The ear alone most safely is believed:
I believe all the Son of God has spoken,
Than Truth's own word there is no truer token.

God only on the Cross lay hid from view;
But here lies hid at once the Manhood too;
And I, in both professing my belief,
Make the same prayer as the repentant thief.

Thy wounds, as Thomas saw, I do not see;
Yet Thee confess my Lord and God to be:
Make me believe Thee ever more and more;
In Thee my hope, in Thee my love to store.

O thou Memorial of our Lord's own dying!
O Bread that Living art and vivifying!
Make ever Thou my soul on Thee to live;
Ever a taste of Heavenly sweetness give.

O loving Pelican! O Jesu, Lord!
Unclean I am, but cleanse me in thy blood;
Of which a single drop, for sinners spilt,
Is ransom for a world's entire guilt.

Jesu! whom for the present veil'd I see,
What I so thirst for, oh, vouchsafe to me:
That I may see thy countenance unfolding,
And may be blest thy glory in beholding.

[*The following is usually sung after every stanza.*]

O Shepherd of the Faithful, O Jesu, gracious be :
Increase the faith of all who put their faith in Thee.

Prose.

Ave, verum corpus natum.

HAIL to Thee! true Body, sprung
From the Virgin Mary's womb!
The same that on the Cross was hung,
And bore for man the bitter doom!

Thou, whose side was pierced, and flow'd
Both with water and with blood;
Suffer us to taste of Thee,
In our life's last agony.

Son of Mary, Jesu blest!
Sweetest, gentlest, holiest!

Hymn for Christmas-Day.

Adeste fideles.

Oh, come! all ye faithful!
 Triumphantly sing!
Come, see in the Manger
 The Angels' dread King!
To Bethlehem hasten!
 With joyful accord;
Oh, hasten! oh, hasten!
 To worship the Lord.

True Son of the Father!
 He comes from the skies;
The womb of the Virgin
 He doth not despise;
To Bethlehem hasten, &c.

Not made but begotten,
   The Lord of all might,
True God of true God,
   True Light of true Light;
To Bethlehem hasten, &c.

Hark! to the Angels!
   All singing in Heaven,
"To God in the highest
   High glory be given."
To Bethlehem hasten, &c.

To Thee, then, O Jesu!
   This day of thy birth,
Be glory and honour
   Through Heaven and earth
True Godhead Incarnate!
   Omnipotent Word!
Oh, hasten! oh, hasten!
   To worship the Lord.

Hymn for Easter-Sunday.

O filii et filiæ.

Ye sons and daughters of the Lord!
The King of glory, King adored,
This day Himself from death restored.

All in the early morning grey
Went holy women on their way,
To see the tomb where Jesus lay.

Of spices pure a precious store
In their pure hands those women bore,
To anoint the sacred Body o'er.

Then straightway one in white they see,
Who saith, " Ye seek the Lord; but He
Is risen, and gone to Galilee."

This told they Peter, told they John;
Who forthwith to the tomb are gone,
But Peter is by John outrun.

That self-same night, while out of fear
The doors were shut, their Lord most dear
To his Apostles did appear.

But Thomas, when of this he heard,
Was doubtful of his brethren's word;
Wherefore again there comes the Lord.

" Thomas, behold my side," saith He;
" My hands, my feet, my body see,
And doubt not, but believe in Me."

When Thomas saw that wounded side,
The truth no longer he denied;
" Thou art my Lord and God!" he cried.

Oh, blest are they who have not seen
Their Lord, and yet believe in Him!
Eternal life awaiteth them.

Now let us praise the Lord most high,
And strive His name to magnify
On this great day, through earth and sky:

Whose mercy ever runneth o'er;
Whom men and Angel Hosts adore;
To Him be glory evermore.

For	*Salutis humanæ sator* . .	see page	100
,,	*Æterne Rex altissime* . .	,,	101
,,	*Pange lingua gloriosi* . .	,,	111
,,	*Tantum ergo sacramentum* .	,,	112
,,	*Sacris solemniis* . . .	,,	113
,,	*Verbum supernum prodiens*	,,	114
,,	*O salutaris Hostia* . .	,,	115
,,	*Stabat Mater dolorosa* .	,,	138
,,	*Lauda Sion Salvatorem* .	,,	236
,,	*Ecce panis angelorum* . .	,,	240

END OF HYMNS AT BENEDICTION OF THE BLESSED SACRAMENT.

HYMNS

FROM THE OFFICE OF THE IMMACULATE CONCEPTION.

AT MATINS.

Salve mundi domina.

Hail, Queen of the Heavens!
Hail, Mistress of earth!
Hail, Virgin most pure,
Of immaculate birth!
Clear Star of the Morning,
In beauty enshrined!
O Lady, make speed
To the help of mankind!

Thee God in the depth
Of eternity chose;
And form'd thee all fair,
As his glorious Spouse;
And call'd thee his Word's
Own Mother to be,
By whom He created
The earth, sky, and sea.

HYMNS FROM THE OFFICE OF

AT PRIME.

Salve Virgo sapiens.

Hail, Virgin most wise!
Hail, Deity's Shrine,
With seven fair pillars
And Table divine!
Preserved from the guilt
Which has come on us all!
Exempt in the womb
From the taint of the Fall!

O new Star of Jacob!
Of Angels the Queen!
O Gate of the Saints!
O Mother of men!
O terrible as
The embattled array!
Be thou of the Faithful
The refuge and stay.

AT TERCE.

Salve arca fœderis.

Hail, Solomon's Throne!
True Ark of the Law!
Fair Rainbow! and Bush
Which the Patriarch saw!
Hail, Gideon's Fleece!
Hail, blossoming Rod!
Samson's sweet Honeycomb!
Portal of God!

Well fitting it was
That a Son so divine
Should preserve from all touch
Of original Sin;
Nor suffer by smallest
Defect to be stain'd
That Mother, whom He
For Himself had ordain'd.

AT SEXT.

Salve Virgo puerpera.

Hail, Virginal Mother!
Hail, Purity's Cell!
Fair Shrine where the Trinity
Loveth to dwell!
Hail, Garden of pleasure!
Celestial Balm!
Cedar of Chastity!
Martyrdom's Palm!

Thou Land set apart
From uses profane,
And free from the curse
Which in Adam began!
Thou City of God!
Thou Gate of the East!
In thee is all grace,
O Joy of the Blest!

AT NONE.

Salve urbs refugii.

Hail, City of refuge!
Hail, David's high tower!
With battlements crown'd,
And girded with power!
Fill'd at thy Conception
With Love and with Light!
The Dragon by Thee
Was shorn of his might.

O Woman most valiant!
O Judith thrice blest!
As David was cherish'd
At Abisag's breast:
As the saviour of Egypt
Upon Rachel's knee;
So the world's great Redeeme
Was fondled by Thee.

AT VESPERS.

Salve horologium.

Hail, Dial of Achaz!
On Thee the true Sun
Told backward the course
Which from old He had run:
And that man might be raised
Submitting to shame,
A little more low
Than the Angels became.

Thou, wrapped in the blaze
Of His infinite Light,
Dost shine as the morn
On the confines of night!
As the Moon on the lost
Through obscurity dawns;
The Serpent's Destroyer!
A Lily 'mid thorns!

AT COMPLINE.

Salve Virgo florens.

Hail, Mother most pure
Hail, Virgin renown'd !
Hail, Queen with the stars
As a diadem crown'd !
Above all the Angels
In glory untold,
Standing next to the King,
In a vesture of gold !

O Mother of mercy !
O Star of the wave !
O Hope of the guilty !
O Light of the grave !
Through Thee may we come
To the Haven of rest ;
And see Heaven's King
In the courts of the Blest

The Commendation.

Supplices offerimus.

These praises and prayers
I lay at thy feet,
O Virgin of virgins!
O Mary most sweet!
Be thou my true guide
Through this pilgrimage here,
And stand by my side
When death draweth near.

END OF HYMNS FROM THE OFFICE OF THE IMMACULATE CONCEPTION.

Feast of St. Anne, Mother of the Blessed Mary.

July 26.

Claræ dici gaudiis.

S<small>POT</small> <small>LESS</small> Anna! Juda's glory!
   Through the Church from East to West,
Every tongue proclaims thy praises,
   Holy Mary's Mother Blest!

     Under thy protecting banner
       Here assembled in thy name,
     Mary's Mother, gracious Anna,
       Grace and help of thee we claim.

Saintly Kings and priestly Sires
   Blended in thy sacred line;
Thou in virtue, all before thee
   Didst excel by grace divine.
              Under thy, &c.

Link'd in bonds of purest wedlock,
   Thine it was for us to bear,
By the favour of High Heaven,
   Our auroral Virgin Star.
                Under thy, &c.

From thy stem in beauty budded
   Ancient Jesse's mystic rod ;
Earth from thee received the Mother
   Of th' Almighty Son of God.
                Under thy, &c.

All the human race benighted
   In the depths of darkness lay ;
When in Anne, it saw the dawning
   Of the long-expected day.
                Under thy, &c.

Honour, glory, virtue, merit,
   Be to Thee, O Virgin's Son !
With the Father and the Spirit,
   While eternal ages run.

Feast of the Nativity of the Blessed Virgin Mary.

September 8.

Aurora quæ Solem paris.

Sweet Morn! thou Parent of the Sun !
   And Daughter of the same !
What joy and gladness, through thy birth,
   This day to mortals came !

Clothed in the Sun I see Thee stand,
   The Moon beneath thy feet ;
The Stars above thy sacred head
   A radiant coronet.

Thrones and Dominions gird Thee round,
   The Armies of the sky ;
Pure streams of glory from Thee flow,
   All bathed in Deity !

Terrific as the banner'd line
   Of battle's dread array!
Before Thee tremble Death and Hell,
   And own thy mighty sway:

While crush'd beneath thy dauntless foot,
   The Serpent writhes in vain;
Smit by a deadly stroke, and bound
   In an eternal chain.

O Mightiest! pray for us, that He
   Who came through Thee of yore
May come to dwell within our hearts,
   And never quit us more.

Praise to the Father, with the Son,
   And Holy Ghost, through Whom
The Word eternal was conceived
   Within the Virgin's womb.

Feast of the Annunciation of the Blessed Virgin Mary.

March 25.

Supernum ales nuntiat.

The Angel spake the word—
"Hail, Thou of women blest!"
From highest Heav'n the Godhead comes,
And fills her virgin breast.

Maiden! how great henceforth
Thy dignity shall be!
The Son of God becomes thine own,
This day conceived by Thee.

This day the Holy Ghost,
From thy all-sinless blood,
Moulds in thy womb that flesh divine
Of the life-giving Word;

Whereby we babes the meat
Of elder ones obtain;
And He, who Angels feeds as God
Feeds men, as God made Man

To Him who, to redeem
  Our race, came down from Heaven,
Praise with the Father evermore,
  And Holy Ghost be given.

Another Hymn for the same Feast.

Quis te canat mortalium?

WHAT mortal tongue can sing thy praise,
  Dear Mother of the Lord?
To Angels only it belongs
  Thy glory to record.

Who born of man can penetrate
  Thy soul's majestic shrine?
Who can thy mighty gifts unfold,
  Or rightly them divine?

Say, Virgin, what sweet force was that,
  Which from the Father's breast
Drew forth his co-eternal Son,
  To be thy bosom's guest?

'Twas not thy guileless faith alone,
   That lifted Thee so high;
'Twas not thy pure seraphic love,
   Or peerless chastity:

But, oh! it was thy lowliness,
   Well pleasing to the Lord,
That made Thee worthy to become
   The Mother of the Word.

Oh, Loftiest!—whose humility
   So sweet it was to see!
That God, forgetful of Himself,
   Abased Himself to Thee!

Praise to the Father, with the Son,
   And Holy Ghost, through Whom
The Word eternal was conceived
   Within the Virgin's womb.

Feast of the Visitation of the Blessed Virgin Mary

July 2.

Quo sanctus ardor te rapit.

WHITHER thus, in holy rapture,
  Royal Maiden, art Thou bent?
Why so fleetly art Thou speeding
  Up the mountain's rough ascent?

Fillèd with eternal Godhead!
  Glowing with the Spirit's flame!
Love it is that bears Thee onward,
  And supports thy tender frame.

Lo! thine aged cousin claims Thee,
  Claims thy sympathy and care;
God her shame from her hath taken;
  He hath heard her fervent prayer.

Blessed Mothers! joyful meeting!
  Thou in her, the hand of God,
She in Thee, with lips inspired,
  Owns the Mother of her Lord.

As the sun his face concealing,
  In a cloud withdraws from sight,
So in Mary' then lay hidden
  He who is the world's true light.

Honour, glory, virtue, merit,
  Be to Thee, O Virgin's Son!
With the Father and the Spirit,
  While eternal ages run.

Feast of the Purification of the Blessed Virgin Mary.

February 2.

Templi sacratas pande Sion fores.

O Sion! open wide thy gates;
  Let figures disappear;
A Priest and Victim both in one,
  The Truth Himself is here.

No more the simple flock shall bleed.—
   Behold the Father's Son
Himself to His own Altar comes
   For sinners to atone.

Conscious of hidden Deity,
   The lowly Virgin brings
Her new-born babe with two young doves,
   Her tender offerings.

The hoary Simeon sees at last
   His Lord so long desired,
And hails, with Anna, Israel's hope,
   With sudden rapture fired.

But silent knelt the Mother blest
   Of the yet silent Word;
And pondering all things in her heart,
   With speechless praise adored.

Praise to the Father with the Son,
   And Holy Spirit be;
Praise to the blessed Three in One,
   Through all eternity.

Feast of the Assumption of the Blessed Virgin Mary.

August 15.

O vos ætherei plaudite cives.

Rejoice, O ye Spirits and Angels on high !
   This day the pure Mother of Love.
By death was set free ; and ascending the sky,
Was welcomed by Jesus, with triumph and joy,
   To the Courts of his glory above.

O Virgin divine ! what treasures are thine!
   What power and splendour untold !
With flesh thou hadst clothed the Lord of all
     might ;—
He clothes Thee in turn with his infinite light,
   And a vesture of radiant gold.

He, who on thy breast found nurture and rest,
   Is now thy ineffable Food ;   [ceal'd,
And He, who from Thee in the flesh lay con-
Now gives Thee, beholding his glory reveal'd,
   To drink from the fulness of God.

Through thy Virginal womb what graces have
    come !
  What glories encompass thy throne !
Where next to thy son, thou sittest a Queen,
Exalted on high, above Angels and men !
  Inferior to Godhead alone !

Then hear us, we pray, on this blessed Day ;
  Remember we also are thine ;
And deign for thy children with Jesus to plead
That He may forgive us, and grant us in need
  His strength and protection divine.

All praise to the Father, who chose for his
    Son
  A Mother, the daughter of Eve ;
All praise to the glorious Child of her womb ;
All praise to the infinite Spirit, by Whom
  Her glory it was to conceive !

Hymn from the Responsory of St. Joseph.

Quicunque sanus vivere.

To all who would holily live,
    To all who would happily die,
St. Joseph is ready to give
    Sure guidance and help from on high.

Of Mary the Spouse undefiled,
    Just, holy, and pure of all stain,
He asks of his own Foster-child;
    And needs but to ask to obtain.

[Here the first stanza is repeated.]

To all who would holily live, &c.

In the manger that Child he adored,
    And nursed Him in exile and flight;
Him, lost in his boyhood, deplored;
    And found with amaze and delight.
            To all, &c.

The Maker of Heaven and Earth
    By the labour of Joseph was fed;
The Son by ineffable birth
    Submissive to Joseph was made.
            To all, &c.

And when his last hour drew nigh,
    Oh, full of all joy was his breast,
Seeing Jesus and Mary close by,
    As he tranquilly slumber'd to rest,
            To all, &c.

All praise to the Father above;
    All praise to the infinite Son;
All praise to the Spirit of love;
    While the days of eternity run.

Hymn from the Responsory of St. Peter.

Si vis Patronum quærere.

Seek ye a Patron to defend
   Your cause?—then, one and all,
Without delay upon the Prince
   Of the Apostles call.

   Blest Holder of the heavenly Keys
     Thy prayers we all implore:
   Unlock to us the sacred bars
     Of Heaven's eternal door.

By penitential tears thou didst
   The path of life regain;
Teach us with thee to weep our sins,
   And wash away their stain.
        Blest Holder, &c.

The Angel touch'd thee, and forthwith
   Thy chains from off thee fell;
Oh, loose us from the subtle coils
   That link us close with Hell.
           Blest Holder, &c.

Firm Rock whereon the Church is based!
   Pillar that cannot bend!
With strength endue us; and the Faith
   From heresy defend.
           Blest Holder, &c.

Save Rome, which from the days of old
   Thy blood hath sanctified;
And help the nations of the earth,
   That in thy help confide.
           Blest Holder, &c.

Oh, worshipp'd by all Christendom!
   Her realms in peace maintain;
Let no contagion sap her strength,
   No discord rend in twain.
           Blest Holder, &c.

The weapons, which our ancient foe
   Against us doth prepare,
Crush thou; nor suffer us to fall
   Into his deadly snare.
            Blest Holder, &c.

Guard us through life; and in that hour
   When our last fight draws nigh,
O'er Death, o'er Hell, o'er Satan's power,
   Gain us the victory.
            Blest Holder, &c.

Praise to the Lord and Father be;
   Praise to the Son who rose;
Praise to the Spirit Paraclete;
   While age on ages flows.
            Blest Holder, &c.

Hymn from the Responsory of St. Paul

Pressi malorum pondere.

ALL ye who groan, beneath
  A load of ills oppress'd!
Intreat St. Paul, and he will pray
  The Lord to give you rest.

  O Victim, dear to Heaven!
  O Paul, thou Teacher true!
Thou love and joy of Christendom!
  To thee for help we sue.

Pierced with the flame of love
  Descending from on high;
'Twas thine to preach the Faith, that once
  Thou soughtest to destroy.
              O Victim, &c.

Nor toil, nor threaten'd death,
  Nor tempest, scourge, or chain,
Could from th' Assembly of the Saints
  Thy loving heart detain.
             O Victim, &c.

Oh, by that quenchless love
  Which burnt in thee of yore!
Take pity on our miseries;
  Our fainting hope restore.
             O Victim, &c.

True Champion of the Lord!
  Crush thou the schemes of Hell;
And with adoring multitudes
  The sacred temples fill.
             O Victim, &c.

Through thy prevailing prayer,
  May Charity abound;
Sweet Charity, which knows no ill,
  Which nothing can confound,
             O Victim, &c.

To earth's remotest shores
May one same Faith extend;
And thy epistles through all climes
Their blessed perfume send.
O Victim, &c.

Grant us the will and power
To serve Thee, God of might!
Lest wavering still, and unprepared,
We sink in depths of night.
O Victim, &c.

Praise to the Father be;
Praise to the Son who rose;
Praise to the Spirit Paraclete;
While age on ages flows.
O Victim, &c.

Hymn from the Responsory of St. Pius the Fifth.

Belli tumultus ingruit.

Wars and tumults fill the earth;
    Men the fear of God despise;
Retribution, vengeance, wrath,
    Brood upon the angry skies.

    Holy Pius! Pope sublime!
    Whom, in this most evil time,
    Whom, of Saints in bliss, can we
    Better call to aid than thee?

None more mightily than thou,
    Hath, by holy deed or word,
Through the spacious earth below
    Spread the glory of the Lord.
              oly Pius, &c.

Thine it was, O Pontiff brave!
　　Pontiff of eternal Rome!
From barbaric yoke to save
　　Terror-stricken Christendom.
　　　　　Holy Pius, &c.

When Lepanto's Gulf beheld,
　　Strewn upon its bosom fair,
Turkey's countless navy yield
　　To the power of thy prayer:
　　　　　Holy Pius, &c.

Who meanwhile, with prophet eye,
　　Didst the distant battle see;
And announce to standers by
　　That same moment's victory
　　　　　Holy Pius, &c.

Mightier now and glorified!
　　Hear the suppliant cry we pour;
Crush rebellion's haughty pride;
　　Quell the din of rising war.
　　　　　Holy Pius, &c.

At thy prayer may golden peace
   Down to earth descend again ;
Licence, discord, trouble cease ;
   Justice, truth, and order reign.
            ·Holy Pius, &c.

To the Lord of endless days,
   One Almighty Trinity ;
Sempiternal glory, praise,
   Honour, might, and blessing be.
            Holy Pius, &c.

Feast of St. Stephen the Protomartyr.

December 26.

O qui tuo dux Martyrum.

O CAPTAIN of the Martyr Host !
   O peerless in renown !
Not from the fading flowers of earth
   Weave we for thee a crown.

The stones that smote thee, in thy blood
   Made beauteous and divine,
All in a halo heavenly bright
   About thy temples shine.

The scars upon thy sacred brow
   Throw beams of glory round ;
The splendours of thy bruisèd face
   The very sun confound.

Oh, earliest Victim sacrificed
   To thy dear Victim Lord !
Oh, earliest witness to the Faith
   Of thy Incarnate God !

Thou to the heavenly Canaan first
   Through the Red Sea didst go,
And to the Martyrs' countless host,
   Their path of glory show.

Erewhile a servant of the poor,
   Now at the Lamb's high Feast,
In blood-empurpled robe array'd,
   A welcome nuptial guest !

To Jesus, born of Virgin bright,
   Praise with the Father be;
Praise to the Spirit Paraclete,
   Through all eternity.

Feast of St. John the Evangelist.

December 27.

Quæ dixit, egit, pertulit.

THE life which God's Incarnate Word
   Lived here below with men,
Three blest Evangelists record
   With Heav'n-inspired pen:

John penetrates on eagle wing
   The Father's dread abode;
And shows the mystery wherein
   The world subsists with God.

Pure Saint! upon his Saviour's breast
    Invited to recline,
'Twas thence he drew, in moments blest,
    His knowledge all divine :

There too, with that angelic love
    Did he his bosom fill,
Which, once enkindled from above,
    Breathes in his pages still.

Oh, dear to Christ !—to thee upon
    His Cross, of all bereft,
Thou Virgin soul ! the Virgin Son
    His Virgin Mother left.

To Jesus, born of Virgin bright,
    Praise with the Father be ;
Praise to the Spirit Paraclete,
    Through all eternity.

Another Hymn for the same Feast.

Jussu tyranni pro fide.

An exile for the Faith
Of thy Incarnate Lord,
Beyond the stars,—beyond all space,
Thy soul unprison'd soar'd:

There saw in glory Him
Who liveth, and was dead;
There Juda's Lion, and the Lamb
That for our ransom bled:

There of the kingdom learnt
The mysteries sublime,
How, sown in Martyrs' blood, the Faith
Should spread from clime to clime.

There the new City, bathed
In her dear Spouse's light,
Pure seat of bliss, thy spirit saw,
And gloried in the sight.

Now to the Lamb's clear fount,
  To drink of life their fill
Thou callest all ;—O Lord, in me
  This blessed thirst instil.

To Jesus, Virgin-born,
  Praise with the Father be ;
Praise to the Spirit Paraclete,
  Through all eternity.

Hymn to Jesus.

Jesu nostra Redemptio.

O Jesu! our Redemption!
  Loved and desired with tears!
God, of all worlds Creator!
  Man, in the close of years!

What wondrous pity moved Thee
  To make our cause thine own
And suffer death and torments,
  For sinners to atone!

O thou, who piercing Hades,
   Thy captives didst unchain!
Who gloriously ascendedst
   Thy Father's Throne again

Subdue our many evils
   By mercy all divine;
And comfort with thy presence
   The hearts that for Thee pine.

Be thou our joy, O Jesu!
   In whom our prize we see;
Always through all the ages,
   In Thee our glory be.

Hymn to the Holy Ghost.

Veni Creator Spiritus.

Come, O Creator Spirit!
   Visit this soul of thine;
This heart of thy creating
   Fill Thou with grace divine.

HYMN TO THE HOLY GHOST.

Who Paraclete art call'd!
    The gift of God above!
Pure Unction! holy Fire!
    And Fount of life and love

Finger of God's right hand!
    The Father's promise true
Who sevenfold gifts bestowest
    Who dost the tongue endow!

Pour love into our hearts;
    Our senses touch with light;
Make strong our human frailty
    With thy supernal might.

Cast far our deadly Foe;
    Thy peace in us fulfil;
So, Thee before us leading,
    May we escape each ill.

The Father, and the Son,
    Through Thee may we receive;
In Thee, from Both proceeding,
    Through endless time believe.

Praise to the Father be;
   Praise to the Son who rose;
And praise to Thee, blest Spirit!
   While age on ages flows.

Hymn for Sunday Morning.
Ad templa nos rursus vocat.

AGAIN the Sunday morn
   Calls us to prayer and praise;
Waking our hearts to gratitude
   With its enlivening rays.

But Christ yet brighter shone,
   Quenching the morning beam;
When triumphing from death He rose,
   And raised us up with Him.

When first the world sprang forth,
   In majesty array'd,
And bathed in streams of purest light;—
   What power was there display'd!

HYMN FOR SUNDAY MORNING.

But oh, what love!—when Christ,
  For our transgressions slain,
Was by th' Eternal Father crown'd
  For us with life again.

His new-created world
  The mighty Maker view'd,
With thousand lovely tints adorn'd;
  And straight pronounced it good.

But oh! much more He joy'd
  That self-same world to see,
Wash'd in the Lamb's all-saving Blood,
  From its impurity.

Nature each day renews
  Her beauty evermore;
Whence to God's hidden Majesty,
  The soul is taught to soar.

But Christ, the Light of all,
  The Father's Image blest,
Gives us to see our God Himself
  In Flesh made manifest.

Blest Trinity! vouchsafe
  That to thy guidance true,
What Thou forbiddest, we may shun:
  What Thou commandest, do.

Hymn of St. Francis Xavier.

O Deus, ego amo Te.

My God, I love Thee, not because
  I hope for Heav'n thereby:
Nor because they, who love Thee not,
  Must burn eternally.

Thou, O my Jesus, Thou didst me
  Upon the Cross embrace;
For me didst bear the nails and spear,
  And manifold disgrace;

And griefs and torments numberless,
  And sweat of agony;
E'en death itself—and all for one
  Who was thine enemy.

Then why, O blessed Jesu Christ!
  Should I not love Thee well;
Not for the sake of winning Heaven,
  Or of escaping Hell:

Not with the hope of gaining aught
  Not seeking a reward;
But, as Thyself hast loved me,
  O ever-loving Lord?

E'en so I love Thee, and will love,
  And in thy praise will sing;
Solely because Thou art my God,
  And my eternal King.

ENGLISH INDEX.

	PAGE
Above the starry spheres	104
Again the slowly circling year	106
Again the Sunday morn	293
All ye who groan, beneath	280
All ye who seek a comfort sure	121
All ye who seek, in hope and love	167
An exile for the Faith	289
Ark of the Covenant! not that	119
At the Cross her station keeping	138
Bathed in eternity's all-beauteous beam	159
Bethlehem! of noblest cities	54
Blest Guardian of all virgin souls	179
Christ's peerless crown is pictured in	69
Come, darkness, spread o'er Heav'n thy pall	171
Come, Holy Ghost, and through each heart	10
Come, O Creator Spirit blest	103
Come, O Creator Spirit	291
Daughter of Sion! cease thy bitter tears	61
Daughters of Sion! royal maids	68
Dear Crown of all the Virgin choir	221
Dear Herald of our King! thou didst	182
Dear Maker of the starry skies	43
Down in adoration falling	113

ENGLISH INDEX.

	PAGE
Dread Framer of the earth and sky	6
Eternal Glory of the heavens	31
Faithful Cross, O Tree all beauteous	233
Father of lights! one glance of Thine	162
Flowers of martyrdom all hail	52
Forth comes the Standard of the King	89
Forth let the long procession stream	83
Forth to the paschal Victim, Christians, bring	233
From highest Heaven, the Father's Son	227
From the far-blazing gate of morn	49
From the Truth thy soul to turn	143
Hail thou Star of ocean	197
Giver of life, eternal Lord	193
Glory and praise to Thee, Redeemer blest	231
Glory of Iberia's throne	142
God, in whom all grace doth dwell	173
Hail, City of refuge	259
Hail, Dial of Achaz	260
Hail, Mother most pure	261
Hail, O Queen of Heaven, enthroned	39
Hail, Queen of the Heavens	255
Hail, Solomon's throne	257
Hail, Spear and Nails! erewhile despised	76
Hail to Thee! true Body, sprung	249
Hail, Virginal Mother	258
Hail, Virgin most wise	256
Hail, wounds! which through eternal years	87
Hark! an awful voice is sounding	46
He who once, in righteous vengeance	85
His sacred feet with tears of agony	164
Holy Mother, pierce me through	140
Holy Spirit! Lord of light	234

ENGLISH INDEX. 299

	PAGE
In caves of the lone wilderness thy youth	156
Jerusalem, thou City blest	225
Jesu! as though Thyself wert here	82
Jesu, brightness of the Father	188
Jesu, Creator of the world	116
Jesu! eternal Truth sublime	219
Jesu, Redeemer of the world	48
Jesu! the very thought of Thee	56
Joseph, our certain hope below	136
Joseph, pure Spouse of that immortal Bride	134
Joy to thee, O Queen of Heaven	39
Laud we the Saint most sweet	223
Lead us, great teacher Paul, in wisdom's ways	129
Let old things pass away	113
Let us arise and watch ere dawn of light	5
Lift to the skies, great Rome, Martina's name	130
Light of the soul, O Saviour blest	168
Lo, fainter now lie spread the shades of night	8
Lo! how the savage crew	118
Lord of all power! at whose command	28
Lord of eternal purity	24
Lord of eternal truth and might	11
Lord of immensity sublime	17
Lo! upon the altar lies	240
Maker of men! who First and Sole	32
Martyr of unconquered might	209
Mother of Almighty God	178
Mother of Christ! hear thou thy people's cry	38
Mother of mercy, hail, O gracious Queen	40
Mother of our Lord and Saviour	152
My God, I love Thee, not because	295
Nigher still, and still more nigh	241

	PAGE
Noble Champion of the Lord	148
Now at the Lamb's high royal feast,	94
Now daily shines the sun more fair	207
Now doth the fiery sun decline	36
Now doth the fiery sun decline	108
Now doth the sun ascend the sky	9
Now let the earth with joy resound	202
Now let us sit and weep	63
Now, while the herald bird of day	19
Now with the fast-departing light	37
Now with the rising golden dawn	27
Now with the slow-revolving year	72
O blessed Saint, of snow-white purity	158
O blest Creator of the light	13
O blest Creator of the world	22
O bounteous Framer of the globe	21
O Captain of the Martyr Host	285
O Christ! the beauty of the angel worlds	133
O Christ, the glory of the Angel choirs	190
O Christ, thy guilty people spare	191
O cruel Herod! why thus fear	53
O'erwhelmed in depths of woe	66
Ofttimes, when hemmed around by hostile arms	150
O glory and high boast	184
O Godhead hid, devoutly I adore Thee	247
Oh, come! all ye faithful	250
Oh, turn those blessed points, all bathed	77
O Jesu! born of Virgin bright	45
O Jesu! King most wonderful	57
O Jesu! life-spring of the soul	145
O Jesu! our Redemption	290
O Jesu! Thou the beauty art	58

	PAGE
O Queen of all the Virgin choir	200
O saving Victim! opening wide	115
O Sion! open wide thy gates	271
O Thou eternal King most high	101
O Thou eternal Source of love	33
O Thou eternal Source of love	109
O Thou, of all thy warriors Lord	208
O Thou pure light of souls that love	100
O Thou, the Father's Image blest	15
O Thou, the Heaven's eternal King	96
O Thou, the Martyrs' glorious King	214
O Thou, thy Mother's Maker, hail	222
O Thou, true life of all that live	12
O Thou, who dost all Nature sway	29
O Thou, who dost all Nature sway	110
O Thou, who thine own Father's breast	45
Our limbs with tranquil sleep refreshed	14
Peter, blest Shepherd! hearken to our cry	128
Peter, whatever thou shalt bind on earth	127
Praise we those ministers celestial	174
Protect thy native City, Spirit blest	132
Pure Light of light! eternal Day	18
Pure, meek, with soul serene	160
Redeemer blest of all who live	217
Rejoice, O ye Spirits and Angels on high	273
Remember, O Creator Lord	201
Riches and regal throne, for Christ's dear sake	161
Ruler of the dread Immense	175
Saint of sweetest majesty	187
See from on high, arrayed in truth and grace	60
Seek ye a Patron to defend	277
See! where in shame the God of glory hangs	65

	PAGE
Sing, my tongue, the Saviour's glory	91
Sing, my tongue, the Saviour's glory	111
Sing we the Martyrs blest	213
Sing we the peerless deeds of martyred Saints	211
Sion, lift thy voice, and sing	236
Son of the Highest! deign to cast	164
Spotless Anna! Juda's glory	263
Star of Jacob, ever beaming	181
Sweet Morn! thou Parent of the Sun	265
The agonizing hooks, the rending scourge	131
The Angel spake the word	267
The Confessor of Christ, from shore to shore	216
The darkness fleets, and joyful earth	74
The dawn is sprinkling in the East	35
The dawn was purpling o'er the sky	98
The glories of that sacred Winding Sheet	78
The golden star of morn	149
The life which God's Incarnate Word	287
The Lord commands; and, lo, his iron chains	166
The Lord's eternal gifts	204
The Lord, whom earth, and air, and sea	199
The pall of night o'ershades the earth	26
The Saviour left high Heaven to dwell	177
These praises and prayers	262
The Word, descending from above	114
This day, beneath the form	183
This day the glorious Trinity	3
This day the wondrous mystery	80
Thou loving Maker of mankind	70
Thus did Christ to perfect manhood	93
Thy body with long fastings worn	186
To all who would holily live	275

	PAGE
To be the Lamb's celestial bride	154
To Christ, the Prince of Peace	123
Unconquered Martyr of his God	146
Unloose, great Baptist, our sin-fetter'd lips	155
Virgin of all virgins best	141
Wars and tumults fill the earth	283
What a sea of tears and sorrow	169
What mortal tongue can sing thy praise	268
What tongue, illustrious Spear, can duly sound	75
When Christ, by his own servants slain	205
When it reached the tyrant's ear	51
Whither thus, in holy rapture	270
Worshipp'd throughout the Church to earth's far ends	137
Ye mist and darkness, cloud and storm	23
Ye sons and daughters of the Lord	252

LATIN INDEX.

	PAGE
Adeste fideles	250
Adora Te devote latens Deitas	247
Ad regias agni dapes	94
Ad templa nos rursus vocat	293
Æterna Christi munera	204
Æterna cœli gloria	31
Æterne Rector siderum	175
Æterne rerum conditor	6
Æterne Rex altissime	101
Ales diei nuntius	19
Alma Redemptoris Mater	38
Alto ex Olympi vertice	227
Antra deserti teneris sub annis	156
A solis ortus cardine	49
Aspice infami Deus ipse ligno	65
Aspice ut Verbum Patris a supernis	60
Athleta Christi nobilis	148
Auctor beate sæculi	116
Audi benigne Conditor	70
Audit tyrannus anxius	51
Aurora cœlum purpurat	96
Aurora jam spargit polum	35

LATIN INDEX.

	PAGE
Aurora quæ Solem poris	265
Ave maris stella	197
Ave Regina cœlorum	39
Ave, verum corpus natum	249
Beata nobis gaudia	106
Beate Pastor Petre clemens accipe	128
Belli tumultus ingruit	283
Christe, sanctorum decus angelorum	133
Christe, sanctorum decus angelorum	190
Christo profusum sanguinem	213
Claræ diei gaudiis	263
Cœlestis Agni nuptias	154
Cœlestis urbs Jerusalem	225
Cœli Deus sanctissime	24
Cœlitum Joseph decus atque nostræ	136
Cœlo Redemptor prætulit	177
Consors paterni luminis	18
Cor arca legem continens	119
Corpus domas jejuniis	186
Creator alme siderum	43
Crudelis Herodes Deum	53
Crux fidelis inter omnes	233
Custodes hominum psallimus angelos	174
Decora lux æternitatis auream	159
Deus tuorum militum	208
Dies iræ dies illa	241
Domare cordis impetus Elizabeth	160
Dum nocte pulsa Lucifer	149
Ecce jam noctis tenuatur umbra	8
Ecce panis angelorum	240
Egregie doctor Paule mores instrue	129
En clara vox redarguit	46

	PAGE
En ut superba criminum	118
Exite Sion filiæ	68
Ex more docti mystico	72
Exultet orbis gaudiis	202
Festivis resonent compita vocibus	83
Fortem virili pectore	223
Gentis Polonæ gloria	184
Gloria, laus, et honor	231
Gloriam sacræ celebremus omnes	78
Hæc est dies qua candidæ	183
Hominis superne conditor	32
Immense cœli conditor	17
Invicte Martyr unicum	209
Ira justa Conditoris	85
Iste Confessor Domini colentes	216
Iste quem læti colimus fideles	137
Jam Christus astra ascenderat	104
Jam lucis orto sidere	9
Jam sol recedit igneus	36
Jam sol recedit igneus	108
Jam toto subditus vesper eat polo	171
Jesu corona celsior	219
Jesu corona Virginum	221
Jesu decus angelicum	58
Jesu dulcis amor meus	82
Jesu dulcis memoria	56
Jesu nostra Redemptio	290
Jesu Redemptor omnium	46
Jesu Redemptor omnium	217
Jesu Rex admirabilis	57
Jussu tyranni pro fide	269
Lauda Sion Salvatorem	236

	PAGE
Legis figuris pingitur	69
Lucis Creator optime	13
Lustra sex qui jam peregit	93
Lux alma Jesu mentium	168
Lux ecce surgit aurea	27
Magnæ Deus potentiæ	28
Maria castis osculis	164
Martinæ celebri plaudite nomini	130
Martyr Dei Venantius	146
Memento rerum Conditor	201
Miris modis repente liber ferrea	166
Mærentes oculi spargite lachrymas	63
Mysterium mirabile	80
Nocte surgentes vigilemus omnes	5
Non illam cruciaus ungula non feræ	131
Nox atra rerum contegit	26
Nox et tenebræ et nubila	23
Nullis te genitor blanditiis trahit	143
Nunc Sancte nobis Spiritus	10
O Deus, ego amo Te	295
O filii et filiæ	252
O gloriosa Virginum	200
O nimis felix meritique celsi	158
Opes decusque regium reliqueras	161
O qui tuo dux Martyrum	285
O quot undis lachrymarum	169
O salutaris Hostia	115
O sola magnarum urbium	54
O Sol salutis intimis	74
O stella Jacob fulgida	181
O vos ætherei plaudite cives	273
Pange lingua gloriosi	91

LATIN INDEX.

	PAGE
Pange lingua gloriosi	111
Paschale mundo gaudium	207
Pater superni luminis	162
Placare, Christe, servulis	191
Præclara custos virginum	179
Pressi malorum pondere.	280
Primo die quo Trinitas	3
Quæ dixit, egit, pertulit	287
Quænam lingua tibi, O Lancea, debitas	75
Quem terra, pontus, sidera	199
Quicunque Christum quæritis.	167
Quicunque certum quæritis	121
Quicunque sanus vivere	275
Quis te canat mortalium?	268
Quodcunque in orbe nexibus revinxeris	127
Quo sanctus ardor te rapit	270
Rector potens, verax Deus	11
Regali solio fortis Iberiæ	142
Regina cœli lætare	39
Regis superni nuntia	182
Rerum Creator optime	22
Rerum Deus tenax vigor	12
Rex gloriose martyrum	214
Rex sempiterne cœlitum	96
Sacris solemniis juncta sint gaudia	113
Sæpe dum Christi populus	150
Sævo dolorum turbine	66
Salutis æternæ dator	193
Salutis humanæ Sator	100
Salve arca fœderis	257
Salve horologium	260
Salve mundi domina	255

LATIN INDEX.

	PAGE
Salve, Regina, Mater misericordiæ	40
Salve urbs refugii	259
Salve Virgo florens	261
Salve Virgo puerpera	258
Salve Virgo sapiens	256
Salvete Christi vulnera	87
Salvete Clavi et Lancea	76
Salvetes flores martyrum	52
Sancta Mater istud agas	140
Sanctorum meritis inclyta gaudia	211
Si vis Patronum quærere	277
Somno refectis artubus	14
Splendor paternæ gloriæ	15
Stabat Mater dolorosa	138
Summæ Deus clementiæ	173
Summæ Parens clementiæ	33
Summæ Parens clementiæ	109
Summi Parentis filio	123
Summi Parentis Unice	164
Supernum ales nuntiat	267
Supplices offerimus	262
Tantum ergo Sacramentum	113
Te deprecante corporum	187
Telluris alme conditor	21
Te lucis ante terminum	37
Te Mater alma Numinis	178
Templi sacratas pande Sion fores	271
Te Joseph celebrent agmina cœlitum	134
Te Redemptoris Dominique nostri	152
Te splendor et virtus Patris	145
Tibi Christe splendor Patris	188
Tinctam ergo Christi sanguine	77

LATIN INDEX.

	PAGE
Tristes erant Apostoli	205
Tu natale solum protege, tu bonæ	132
Tu Trinitatis Unitas	29
Tu Trinitatis Unitas	110
Ut queant laxis resonare fibris	155
Veni Creator Spiritus	103
Veni Creator Spiritus	291
Veni Sancte Spiritus	234
Venit e Cœlo Mediator alto	61
Verbum supernum prodiens	45
Verbum supernum prodiens	114
Vexilla Regis prodeunt	89
Victimæ Paschali laudes	233
Virgo virginum præclara	141
Virginis Proles Opifexque matris	222

FINIS.

www.ingramcontent.com/pod-product-compliance
Lightning Source LLC
Chambersburg PA
CBHW031852220426
43663CB00006B/590